Being and Loving

Being and Loving

ALTHEA HORNER

Foreword by Howard Halpern

JASON ARONSON INC.
Northvale, New Jersey
London

Copyright © 1986, 1978 by Althea J. Horner

Library of Congress Cataloging in Publication Data

Horner, Althea.
  Being and loving.

  Bibliography: p. 139.
  1. Identity (Psychology)   2. Intimacy
  (Psychology)   3. Developmental psychology.
  I. Title.

BF697.H56   158   77-73972

ISBN 0-87668-931-4

Manufactured in the United States of America

To my mother

CELIA NEWMARK GREENWALD

1891–1975
*with gratitude for the
steadfastness of her love
even when I was most unlovable.*

CONTENTS

FOREWORD

I WAS A YOUNG STUDENT, learning about projective testing in a university clinic. I was testing a seven-year-old boy who had been brought to the clinic because his behavior was aggressive and disruptive. He looked as he had been described—tough and surly. As one of the projective tests, I asked him what animal he would like to be. He instantly answered, "A puppy." I asked him why and he responded, "Because puppies are cute and everyone would hold me and pet me." I gave him a piece of paper and told him I would like him to draw the puppy he would like to be. He drew a four-legged animal in side view, and then, beginning at the neck, started to draw little dashes coming out of the line of the puppy's back, saying, "This is his hair." As he drew each dash, it got longer, so that by the time he got to the rear end of his animal, they were quite long. He looked at it and said, "No, this isn't a puppy; it's a porcupine. It has these long needles to keep people away so he won't get hurt."

It was all there: his desire for warmth and stroking, his fear that he would be hurt if he let anyone close enough to give him that warmth, and his use of behavioral quills to keep others at a distance. And what was also implied was that already, in his young life, he had had experiences with closeness that brought him sufficient pain to cause him to choose quills over closeness.

If we were to move forward on the boy's time track and, if there were no modifying intervening factors, see him ten years later, or twenty years later, we would expect to see a rather offensive, probably belligerent adolescent or young man with little trace of softness, with little genuine intimacy with anyone, and perhaps, by then, without even the conscious memory that once he longed for loving. If we could probe deep enough, we would certainly find that the yearning for warmth is still there. But now it is buried beneath a behavioral repertoire that keeps him distanced and split off from his deepest needs.

This conflict between the longing for love and intimacy and the fear of some type of pain or loss of self if we permit ourselves to get close enough to get this warmth is an ancient human dilemma that bedevils most of us. Not all of us turn into porcupines as ways of distancing—some of us become moles or skunks. Others of us feel the longing so powerfully that we do not distance at all, but become lifetime puppies, kittens or leeches. None of these choices are very satisfactory. All do violence to some basic part of us.

In Dr. Horner's book, she indicates what type of early experiences, particularly early mothering experiences, have led us to make the choices we have made in the attempt to resolve our own problem of being and loving. We have, in a way, made this "decision" very early, and it becomes a decision that we tend to adhere to stubbornly despite its obviously self-defeating repercussions.

Can we choose differently now? In addressing herself to this question, Dr. Horner is dealing with an issue that is both psychologically and philosophically troubling, namely, to what extent do we have the freedom to change a basic pattern of being that has been stamped into our experiences and engraved on our neurones when we were so very young and malleable? It is the old question of determinism versus free will, and Dr. Horner offers no easy solutions. Just as she sees the tragic waste of selfhood in those love addicts who function only in a symbiotically dependent relationship with another person, she decries the attempt to escape such dependence by a running in the opposite direction toward doing one's own thing with little regard for one's responsibility to others or the beauty of a loving commitment to another person. She reaches, from a developmental framework, a viewpoint similar to Hillel. "If not for me, who will be; but if I am for me alone, then what am I?"

What she offers to those who are unhappy about how they are operating in the dimension of being and loving derives from the work of those psychologists, particularly those from England, whose study of early childhood experience has led to so much understanding of how an individual comes to relate to others in a particular way for the rest of his or her life.

She tells us that, while we cannot rewrite our histories, our awareness of the forces that shaped us, our recognition of the continuing influence of these forces, an awareness of new possibilities and the making of new choices based on this knowledge, can deeply modify our early decisions about being and loving. But she makes it clear that accomplishing this is painful, and that you will confront feelings ranging from depression through terror as you mourn the old and reach for the unknown.

No matter where you find yourself on the being-loving continuum, you will feel no sense of being blamed or denigrated for being there. Dr. Horner understands, with her considerable intellect and breadth of knowledge, the forces that led you to where you are, and she empathizes out of some deeply warm and resonant place within herself with the struggle each person must undertake to be a full, separate, and loving self. These qualities make her an able and caring guide, and make the book both cognitively and affectively nurturing.

HOWARD HALPERN, PH.D

INTRODUCTION

THE QUESTION POSED in this volume is timeless: How can I be in a close relationship and still be me?

The "Me Decade" of the seventies has passed, leaving behind a sense of an experiment that failed. The triumph of self is a hollow victory when it is achieved at the cost of vital connection to another person. Men and women—both young and old—who fled familial entanglements found themselves hungering for something to take the family's place. "Doing their own thing," although exciting at first, left them with no sense of real purpose, no sense of a future toward which to build. Social alienation became personal alienation as the loving human spirit atrophied.

Young people of the 1980s find themselves drawn back to old values and dreams. With the gains made by women, socially and economically, the spirit of revolution is being replaced by a move toward conserving and preserving what was central to the emotional life of preceding generations: love, home, and family. The current freedom of choice brings its own conflicts and dilemmas. Women who opted for careers on a path of supposed self-realization are confronted with the reality of the "biological clock," and some, almost frantically, are seeking to retrieve what was rebelliously discarded.

But the young couples of the eighties are not retreating in disarray. Consolidating the gains of social change, they have found that something else is possible—that one *can* be in a close, loving relationship without surrendering identity. A new sense of "we" is emerging, a joining in that space between the "me" and the "you" where love has actually always existed. In this intermediate arena, where two people truly meet as loving adults, there is an extended, deepened sense of the self, an experience of being that comes only when there is a joining with the self of another. There is no surrender of identity or autonomy; rather, each person is enriched. Something new is created, in the same way that a new and unique being is created when a child comes out of such love.

I have used the terms *being* and *loving* in a particular way: to denote the desired end points of a developmental process that begins at the very start of life. "Loving" does not refer only to the momentary overflowing of good feeling toward someone else. It entails an emotional attachment to another human being, one predicated not only on one's dependency needs, but also on one's valuing and cherishing the other as the real person he or she is. It is an attachment that is constant over time and circumstance. Love does not disappear when there is separation. Love does not die when there is anger.

"Being" refers to that clear and uninterrupted sense of "I am. I exist. I go on." It is the capacity to experience oneself as a separate, real, and whole human being. The self-perception of the individual who has this capacity involves neither overidealization nor undeserved contempt. There is a realistic acceptance and integration of the many diverse qualities that characterize any real person.

The barriers to that wished-for experience of the "we" continue to plague and frustrate many people. This book addresses those barriers in the hope that confronting them and struggling past them will enable some to achieve a new synthesis: a self able to love, to commit, and to share.

ALTHEA J. HORNER

Being and Loving

CHAPTER 1

BEING VERSUS LOVING: THE CORE CONFLICT

CAL HAS BEEN married three times and has had numerous affairs. Drawn by a yearning for warmth and closeness, he enters into each new relationship with all the elation and excitement of "falling in love." For a while, he feels that maybe, just maybe he has found the right woman, the woman who will really give him the love and understanding he needs. But as the relationship progresses and the woman expresses her own emotional needs or wishes, Cal becomes irritated by what he experiences as her demands. He feels burdened and controlled by them. Eventually, the warmth and intimacy that he sought, and thought he had found, are replaced by annoyance and resentment at a relationship that seems to deprive him of his independence. As he sees it now, he cannot be himself if he gets too close.

Elizabeth has always been proud of her capacity to adapt. As a child, when she moved from city to city because of her father's job, she would look over the new situation at school, size up how she would have to act to fit in, and then easily slide into the social niche she picked out for herself. Later this capacity to adapt had helped her to play the roles laid out for her as the wife of a rising young business executive and had enabled her to accept the crises and problems that had come along over the years as part of marriage.

But now after years of being a dutiful wife, concerned mother and P.T.A. member, her world seemed to be crumbling. One evening Bob had told her that he wanted a divorce. Faced with the prospect of being alone, Elizabeth had turned to a women's group for advice and support; but all the talk about goals and careers, about self-assertion and seeking one's own identity had only confronted her with the reality that she had long ago surrendered any sense of who she was in order to fit in, to avoid rejection or criticism, and thus ensure that she would never have to face being alone.

Sara and Leon have been married just over five years. While still planning their marriage, they had decided that Sara would continue to work full time not for the added income but for Sara's sake as a person in her own right. Now both she had Leon have positions at the managerial level in their professions. Intelligent, attractive, and successful, they would seem to be a perfect match for each other. But their weekends alone together are a disaster. When one feels sociable or sexual, the other is too involved in some important project to respond. When one is in a playful mood, the other is depressed. In effect, when one says, "Come close," the other says, "Go away," and vice versa. They each complain of chronic dissatisfaction with the other, but neither is able to break the stalemate.

What we see in the cases of Calvin, Elizabeth, and Sara and Leon are examples of one of the fundamental conflicts of human nature: the conflict between being and loving, which is so often expressed, "How can I achieve love and intimacy with another person without losing my own sense of self, my own identity and independence?"

Many, in fact most, people to some extent attempt to resolve the conflict by sacrificing one to safeguard the other. As in the case of Calvin, some people eschew love to protect their autonomy and sense of self. Others, like Elizabeth, sacrifice their identity or independence in order to preserve a relationship, while people like Sara and Leon seem unable to move in either direction and remain trapped in their own ambivalence.

None of these solutions are very satisfactory or necessarily successful. They are made at a cost that is high in anxiety, loneliness, depression, or unremitting rage; and for many of the men and women who pay the price, "true love" remains elusive.

But what does "love" mean? In the sense that it is used here, it is not familial love between parents and children or brothers and sisters, but the new love of adult life that supersedes those earlier relationships. It entails the realization that love is not a threat to the self, to one's sense of who one is, to one's boundaries and one's autonomy, or something to be bargained for and received in exchange for the core of one's personhood. It involves the capacity to give and care for another in a manner that does not entail the sacrificing of one's identity.

When we applaud, we know that our two hands are separate. Yet they come together in a common enterprise in such a way that we cannot tell which hand claps and which is clapped. The sound they produce can exist only because of the readiness of each to engage the other without concern for which does which.

This is the nature of true love and intimacy, which can only exist between two people whose sense of their own individual separateness and wholeness is secure enough to enable each to engage the other fully, with no fear of loss of self and without concern for who gives and who receives. Few of us realize this ideal perfectly for it rests upon foundations laid down in the formative first three years of life. During this crucial period, the primary mothering person must care for and respond to the child in such a way as to facilitate the establishment of the attachment bond, the emotional connection with the principal caretaker which is the basis for the capacity to love. At the same time the parent must promote individuation, the process of becoming a unique individual. But given the imperfectability of the world and of the men and women who live in it, our parents were unable, unwilling, or just too preoccupied with other demands to provide such careful nurturing of our delicate psyches. Thus the extent to which we succeed in achieving true love and intimacy depends to a large degree on how we deal with problems left over from the very earliest years of life.

The fact that most of us as children differed with respect to the

vigor and persistence of self-expressive behavior adds further to our
adult conflict between being and loving. Some of us were adapters;
others fighters. Persons like Elizabeth who adapted without protest
while growing up were likely to have been viewed as "good" children. As adults, however, they may well find themselves struggling
with issues of identity. Adults who as children fought and were very
likely labelled "bad" may still be paying the price of loss of love or
emotional isolation. Along with the quality of parenting and our
innate temperament, the demands of the developmental process
itself, family, religion, and wider social and cultural values all contribute both to our healthy development and to our conflict.

Although the family is the ideal setting for the development of
both the capacity to love and the capacity to be some families,
headed by parents who themselves have problems and unresolved
conflicts with respect to these very same issues, develop mechanisms
for blocking the emergence of individuality in their members because it is seen as a threat to the stability and continued existence of
the family as a unit.

Consider an adolescent boy whose interests have quite normally
moved from the family to the world of peers and who is labelled
"selfish" for wanting to go to a party rather than staying at home for a
family barbecue. His father tells him he is spoiling the family's good
time. As a result the boy is beset by guilt which, in turn, inhibits his
efforts to graduate out of the family. Even more subtle and powerful
are covert threats of emotional abandonment.

Doris is a thirty-two-year-old executive secretary who lives alone
and suffers from periodic bouts of depression. When she was thir-
teen she was invited for the first time to spend the night at the home
of a friend. She phoned her mother to tell her this and to say that she
would be home the following morning. Her mother replied:

"Who is this?"

"It's Doris."

"I can't hear you. Who is speaking?"

"It's Doris. Your daughter."

"I'm sorry. I still can't hear you."

Discouraged, Doris gave up and mumbled, "Never mind, I'll

come home," to which her mother cheerfully replied, "I'll see you in a little while, darling."

This nonrecognition by her mother as soon as Doris attempted to define herself as separate was a threat to the adolescent's very feelings of existence. So powerful was it that it pulled Doris back within the confines of the family and prevented any further healthy assertion of her self as a separate and autonomous individual. Doris had been subjected to this kind of covert control from the earliest years of her life, and so never developed the sure sense of self that might enable her to oppose her mother later on. The rest of the family aided and abetted the system by showing disapproval whenever she questioned her mother's perfection as a parent.

Before moving on, I want to make it perfectly clear that despite the failure of many families to foster healthy development in their children, the challenge lies in addressing and correcting the failure itself rather than doing away with the family as an institution.

For some people, the role played by the family in producing a conflict between being and loving is intensified by religion. Religious teachings concerning moral and ethical obligations necessarily impose upon the self certain constraints with regard to other people and to one's community. At the same time they contribute to the anxiety and guilt associated with experiencing those aspects of the self which conflict with the rules and values of one's faith. This is particularly true of sexuality. When sexual guilt or anxiety are sufficiently severe, a vital component of the self must be cut off, denied, or repressed ultimately at the cost of one's sense of wholeness.

Beyond certain problems sometimes generated within the family and added to by religious teachings, wider social attitudes and values aggravate the early developmental conflict between being and loving. This is particularly true with respect to male and female sex role expectations. The women's movement's goal of equal political, social, and economic rights is underscored by recognition that, in many instances, the very selfhood of women has been denied in the historical, conventional marital relationship. This would be especially true of those women who, earlier in life, were adapters, women who as little girls and in adolescence conformed to adult expectations. Elizabeth is an example of such a woman. They bring the compliant-child attitude into their marriages, weaving it into the role of wife.

Although men have traditionally held greater social, economic, and political power both in and out of the family, they have the same basic struggle and conflict with respect to being and loving. Perhaps they have a greater tendency to sacrifice loving for being as an outcome of the struggle of the little boy to be a "little man," and to deny the loving relationship with mother. The closeness with her may stand as a threat to his sense of his maleness as well as his need to live up to what is expected of him as a male. The pressure of role expectation on the little girl is just the opposite, however, and she is more likely to stay close to mother for a longer period of time. In this instance, loving takes precedence over being. This is borne out by child development research which reveals, for example, that mothers of little girls between the ages of six and eighteen months handle and talk to their children significantly more than do mothers of little boys.[1]

In his sensitive short story, "I Don't Need You Any More,"[2] Arthur Miller writes of a little boy who angrily spits these words at his mother in his attempt to extricate himself from the web of her overprotection. He wants desperately to be one of the men.

> And suddenly he remembered: "I don't need you any more!" His own words came back, shrill and red with fury. Why was that so terrible? He didn't need her. He could tie his laces now, he could walk forever without getting tired. . . . She didn't want him, why did he have to pretend he wanted her? The horror in it escaped him. Still, it probably was horrible anyway, only he didn't understand why. . . . How fine it would be to sink into the ocean now, he thought. How she would plead with his dead, shut-eyed face to say something.

Mr. Miller conveys beautifully the struggle for selfhood and for manhood in this young boy-child, and shows how in anger at his

1. Susan Goldberg and Michael Lewis, "Play Behavior in the Year-old Infant: Early Sex Differences," *Child Development* 40, no.1 (1969): 21–31.
2. Arthur Miller, *I Don't Need You Any More* (New York: Viking, 1967), p. 15.

mother's frustration of his wish to be, he denies to her and to himself his need and love for her.

Men and women who shut themselves off from feelings of warmth or love in order to protect the integrity of the self ultimately come to feel deprived of those very experiences. The experience of deprivation, in turn, generates anger. Pillow pounding "to get the rage out," as is the fashion in some encounter and therapy situations, is an exercise in futility. What is at issue is not access to rage, which often comes all too readily, but avoidance of attachment. The death fantasy of Miller's character is like many a suicidal fantasy of the angry individual who denies attachment. "I don't need you any more!" is the final scream of rage.

Whether it be the innate developmental conflict between being and loving, the demands and expectations of family, religion, or sex role assignment, the coming together of diverse forces and pressure which oppose the achievement and expression of selfhood has generated a counterforce, a social-psychological movement which can best be described as the "cult of self."

CHAPTER 2

THE CULT OF SELF

THE CURRENT EMPHASIS, both in and out of psychology, on the importance of the self can be traced in part to a concept which first appeared in humanistic psychology. Abraham Maslow,[1] one of the founders of humanistic psychology, hoped to develop a psychology of the whole person which would address itself to what he referred to as "self-actualization." Unfortunately, his terminology has been extracted from his science and transformed into the shallow oversimplification which now stands, in many circles, as a banal pseudoscientific justification for narcissistic self-gratification at the expense of, or in disregard of, other people. At best others are dealt with rather than related to, and self-actualization is equated with denial of the importance of the other in one's life. This is clearly a distortion of Maslow's views. Indeed, in his final book, he describes self-actualizing people as persons who have feelings of belongingness and rootedness, as people who have friends and feel loved and loveworthy.

Such is not the case with the proponents of the cult of self. Their maxim, "If it feels good, do it," suggests rejection of legitimate issues

---

1. A. Maslow, *The Farther Reaches of Human Nature* (New York: Viking, 1971).

of conscience and concern for others. Human values that have to do with what is moral or ethical or even simply decent are considered irrelevant and representative of earlier repressive forces in an individual's life. Objections to such an attitude are put down with "Go fuck yourself," a catchphrase that cuts off any opportunity for true dialogue. Indeed, "doing one's thing," another maxim of those who preach and practice the cult of self, often implies that the other person doesn't count. No book title expresses this and the other tenets of the cult of self more succinctly than *Looking Out for Number One.*

I have no quarrel with the importance of the capacity to stand firm in the face of assault on one's psychological boundaries or with a person's right to define himself and to live according to that definition. However, if this does not lead to the capacity to trust that one can feel whole, integrated and real, *in* a relationship, if it does not open one to the possibility of genuine intimacy, then the self becomes the citadel rather than the center of one's being.

One of the most noticeable characteristics of present society is what seems to be a flight from genuine intimacy. Intimacy with commitment is mistakenly equated with dependency, although the two may clearly go hand in hand and often do. Because of the painful awareness of the binds and costs of dependency, because of the readiness to feel trapped by belongingness or rootedness, intimacy for some has become a threat rather than a promise. But the yearning for it surfaces and reappears, and intimacy games have become an integral part of the encounter group experience. They are an attempt to recapture that which has been thrown away. However, hugging and stroking people we know we will never see again after five o'clock on Sunday afternoon is not intimacy, and come Monday morning, the same loneliness and sense of loss and isolation are back in all their painful intensity.[2]

Because of the anticipated dangers of intimacy with enduring ties, however, conscious concern focuses instead on maintaining separateness. Some individuals turn to assertiveness training as a way to experience and protect the endangered self. Although on one level it does serve toward this end, saying no is not enough.

2. A. Horner, "Self-deception and the Search for Intimacy," *Voices* 6, no. 2 (1971): 34–36.

SAYING NO IS NOT ENOUGH

Although the capacity to say no is an essential guardian of that which is intrinsic to the self, and although it paves the way for acknowledging and expressing the self, no-saying alone will not be enough to establish one's sense of identity. For no-saying is essentially reactive rather than expressive behavior.

Some people live their lives primarily as reactors rather than as initiators. They do not feel real or alive much of the time because they are cut off from that which is intrinsic to the self. Instead they wave highly sensitive antennae about to receive signals as to what is going on with the other person, with a readiness to react to this information in some characteristic ways. Some people's characteristic reaction is negativism. For others it is compliance.

Being encouraged to say no leads the latter type of individual nowhere. For no-saying simply means compliance with a new should. The automatic compliant self may simply be replaced with an equally automatic resistant or negativistic self. This may create an illusion of self-assertion, but it is still a reactive stance. It does not necessarily give access to that which is intrinsic to the self. Sometimes it necessitates renunciation of that which is actually wanted or longed for. For many people the problem is not, "I say yes when I want to say no"; it is, "I say no when I want to say yes."

This dilemma is illustrated by the young woman who observed that when she genuinely felt something positive toward another person and expressed her good feeling, there would be an immediate *inner* shift, and it would suddenly feel as if she were simply trying to please that individual. With this inner shift from, "I'm doing it for me," to, "I'm doing it for you," the good feelings would be replaced with resentment and anger. Her difficulty in differentiating what she wanted from what the other wanted put her in an impossible bind. It also put the other person in a bind, for there could be no way to respond to her that would not in some way make her upset or angry. If the other person responded negatively to her good feelings, or even just ignored them, she would feel rejected. If the other person responded positively, she would feel controlled and angry. Her basic stance in life was a compliant one, and she struggled to emerge from it through its opposite—through negativism.

Rollo May comments, ". . . autonomy and freedom cannot be the domain of a special part of the organism, but must be a quality of the total self—the thinking-feeling-choosing-acting organism."[3] This is the essence of identity, of the sense of self which implies an integration of the many different facets of one's personality. When the wish and longing for love and intimacy are denied, there can be no such integration. When identity is inaccessible or when the real self must be kept in a secret psychological sanctuary, there can be no such integration. When living is a series of reactions to others rather than an expression of that which is inherently and intrinsically part of the self, there can be no such integration. Saying no will not be enough to assure that we can, indeed, be masters of our own fate. The goal is to have the freedom to say yes without losing one's sense of self or one's autonomy, for true intimacy involves both yes and no.

Nor is "Letting it all hang out" what is meant here by being real or, as the humanistic or existential psychologist would put it, being authentic. For being real is something you *experience* rather than something you do.

There are certain inevitable restrictions on our spontaneity simply because we are social beings who must live within an organized society. To the extent we exercise even common courtesy or consideration for others, we are not always being fully spontaneous. We also limit our spontaneity on the basis of realistic consequences of its expression. One may think, but not express, the opinion that one's boss is an SOB. We also limit our spontaneity when we must put feelings aside to meet the requirements of the job. Filling out forms may be a pain, but one does not act upon the wish and impulse to tear them up and file them in the circular file. Even so, we hope we can still *feel* real, remaining in touch with our experience and our own identity, and maintaining a firm sense of our own psychological boundaries.

Access to the real rather than the reactive self is the *sine qua non* for being, and without it loving and intimacy are impossible. When only the reactive self participates in a relationship, the real self remains isolated and lonely. The suicide of "the man who has everything" may sometimes be an expression of that despair.

3. Rollo May, *Love and Will* (New York: Norton, 1969), p. 199.

THE POWER MERCHANTS

Another approach of the cult of self is through power. There is no weekend magic which will bring about the kinds of lasting inner changes that will allow for the ultimate integration of loving with being. Yet certain charismatic leaders imply that they do, indeed, have another brand of magic. Its name is power. The prime example of this is est, although it is characteristic of others as well. These leaders draw upon feelings of helplessness and offer the exhilaration of power in its stead. Although the est training may be designed to "jolt people into a space from which they could then be open to self experience,"[4] one cannot assume that everyone reacts to such jolting in a growth-promoting manner.

The technique itself is based on the power of the authority figure, despite the so-called "agreement" to submit to that authority. Once one has made this agreement, there seem to be two choices open. The first is to resist, and be an "asshole." (An asshole is "what everyone is before he or she knows what is real and what isn't."[5]) The term itself is so pejorative in nature that it is coercive. Who wants to be exposed publicly as an asshole!

The second alternative is to comply, and thus to share in the good feeling of being part of the "in" group. This sense of belonging, based as it is on a smug superiority, provides a heightened sense of self-esteem right off the bat. At the very outset the participant hands over to the leader the power to define reality, despite the message that it is the participant who creates his or her reality. So now the alternatives are: (1) "Yes, I do create my own reality" (accepting the basic premise of the leader), or (2) "I am an asshole" (not accepting this premise). In effect these alternatives say either, "I am all powerful," or, "I am nothing." Thus, the individual is thrust back into the early developmental dilemma of the power pivot (chapter 6). Through exhortation, suggestion, and intimidation, people are brought to accept the premise of power and apparently feel better for it. The question raised here is whether feeling better is necessarily growth. It can also be delusion.

4. Adelaide Bry, *60 Hours That Transform Your Life* (New York: Avon, 1976), p. 203.
5. Ibid., p. 226.

No one likes to feel helpless and afraid. Leaders who themselves exude power and self-confidence imply, in effect, "if you follow me, you can have my power." Their followers renounce their equally unrealistic identities as helpless victims and substitute for them an identification with the all-powerful parent-leader. However, this identity is as unrelated to the real and intrinsic self of the individual as is the reactive self of the no-sayer. Furthermore, such identifications are unstable,[6] that is, they do not become an integral part of the self, but are dependent upon the continuing relationship with the idealized parent figure. In the case of est, this is the est organization itself. Thus est guarantees its own survival as the needed source of power for its members.

The good feeling and sense of power that come out of the we-feeling that is promoted in such settings may give the individual the courage to confront situations and problems formerly avoided. In this manner, growth may be set in motion. But not necessarily. The good feelings may themselves generate so much gratification that the task of becoming a separate, whole, and autonomous man or woman continues to be avoided.

Dr. Leon Festinger's research on attitudes showed how people use a variety of mental mechanisms to reduce conflict between two conflicting attitudes. This conflict is referred to as "cognitive dissonance."[7] People rationalize, perceive selectively, or change one of the attitudes to do away with the discomfort of this dissonance. Question must be raised about the contribution of this mechanism to the changed attitudes of the est participants. The attitude, "I am a person of value (not an asshole)" may conflict with the attitudes put forth by the authoritarian leader as the Truth. A way out of this situation of cognitive dissonance would be to change one's attitude about reality. The alternative would be to deny the basic premise of assholeness. But then, this would only *prove* that one *is* an asshole! According to Dr. Bry, Werner Erhard is an expert in paradox, which he uses well to coerce the outcome he desires. One might wonder if

6. Heinz Kohut, *The Reconstruction of the Self* (New York: International Universities Press, 1977), p. 263.

7. L. L. Festinger, H. W. Riecken and S. Schacter, *When Prophecy Fails* (Minneapolis: University of Minnesota Press, 1956), p. 140.

est could carry out its program *and* eliminate that one factor—the contemptuous, pejorative, and self-esteem annihilating labeling of those who do not comply, who do not see the Truth.

Although est leaders try to screen out individuals who might have a bad reaction to their approach, there are inevitable casualties in any situation which has such a strong emotional impact upon the individual. The growing list of encounter group "casualties" is attributed largely to the effects of such charismatic leaders upon individuals with a shaky sense of self and of their own psychological boundaries.[8] Rather than heighten the person's experience of self, the emotionally laden impingement of both leaders and their enthusiastic followers can further confuse the individual and weaken what sense of self there is.

The autonomy that derives from identifying with the leader who dismisses others with "bullshit" is also illusory, for fundamental to this newfound power to assert the self is the surrender of one's intrinsic and authentic being to the identification with the powerful leader. The political consequences of surrender of self to the powerful leader, with the gratifying feelings of participating in his power, make for bloody reading in the history of humankind.

The field of psychotherapy is both an expression of and a vehicle for social change. Sometimes it may become perverted to mere justification for a return to the self-centeredness of early childhood with its demand for total license and parental indulgence. Whatever the expression of cult of self, it will involve the rejection of certain human and social values, such as that of "generativity," described by Erik Erikson[9] as the capacity for altruistic concern for others. The technique of any psychotherapy cannot be divorced from its goals, and its goals are inevitably determined by the value orientation of the therapist.

There are no quick and easy solutions to the dilemma presented by the equally powerful but often antithetical drives for intimacy and

8. H. B. Roback and S. J. Abramowitz, "Deterioration Effects in Encounter Groups," *American Psychologist* 31, no. 3 (1976): 247–55.

9. Erik Erikson, *Identity: Youth and Crisis* (New York: Norton, 1968), p. 138.

identity—for loving and being. Some people deny the yearning for attachment. Others renounce the self. In the best of all possible worlds, each of us would be able to achieve both and to have to give up neither. Although it offers no simple solutions, this book will enable you to strive, however imperfectly, for ways to resolve your own personal conflict.

The first step in solving the problem of attaining this best of all possible worlds is to define it, to know it, to see where the stumbling places are along the way, to articulate those choices which will have to be made, and to decide what will have to be left behind as well as what is being sought.

Looking back to the very start of life at the developmental path we all have had to follow during the critical, formative years of life, not only sheds light on the nature of the problem as it exists for any one of us today. It also foreshadows what is to come, for all the steps toward this best of all possible worlds are originally laid out in the first three or four years of our psychological development. Some lucky individuals make the trip the first time. Many get stuck in some cul-de-sac along the way and, even as men and women, continue to struggle with the unresolved conflicts. Looking back is a necessary and integral part of moving ahead.

CHAPTER 3

WHY LOOK BACK?

UNDERSTANDING HOW certain aspects of the past have left their mark does not necessarily change the quality of one's life. Explanations such as, "I never developed self-confidence because my father was always criticizing me," or "I was afraid to speak my own mind because my mother was so domineering," can be reassuring insofar as they offer a rationale and justification for self-defeating attitudes and behaviors or for anger and righteous indignation. But insight alone does not help; and this fact has led many psychologists in recent years to favor instead techniques of self-discovery that rely upon the experience of the moment. More and more we find new therapeutic approaches emphasizing the "here and now," with specific prohibition on the search for understanding.

Now it is certainly true that since the past is memory and the future is hope (or dread) this moment in time is the only one we ever really have. It is also true that the past is often used to avoid looking at the present, to protect ourselves from an awareness of immediate pain or conflict, or from the anxieties inherent in change. Blaming our parents is also more comfortable than forcing answers to "What is there about my character, my psychological makeup—the ways in which I relate, the assumptions I make about my self and others, the expectations I hold, the meanings I assign to what I experience, the self-deceptions I practice—which contribute to the continuation of my unhappiness?"

Yet the impact of the past on our basic personality structure is such that we cannot dismiss it out of hand. Our present ways of experiencing and defining ourselves in various relationships and circumstances are an outgrowth of our earliest experiences in the world. What we experience today takes its meaning from the total context of our lives, not just the "here and now." Our reactions to events in our lives are based not only on the objective facts but also on the meaning we give to what we experience.

You are a woman of thirty-two who met an attractive man at a singles club two weeks ago. He said he would call. He didn't. What meaning do you assign to these objective facts?

1. You can't trust anyone to follow through on a promise.
2. There's something about me that drives people away.
3. He was trying to manipulate me to make himself feel good.
4. He must be busy with problems of his own as I am.
5. _____(add your own).

Each one of these intepretations can be directly related to a generalized feeling about the self and about others.

Limited understanding of cause and effect, a tendency to think concretely and egocentrically, and a very limited capacity to understand how others work psychologically, make a child prone to distorted conclusions about the self and about others which persist as the core of our basic premises for adult life. To try to change only within the context of the here and now necessitates denial of the existence not only of the conclusions of childhood but of the whole rational superstructure tailored to fit them which a person develops over a lifetime.

Looking back and reviewing the evidence, as it were, enables an adult to understand how his psychological makeup came about and how it had survival value for the helpless child he once was. Adult intellect, strength, and understanding of reality are brought to bear upon meanings constructed before one had language or logic often with the result that the relationship between present experience and developmental forerunners becomes fairly obvious. This is especially true when the early events took place within the time of conscious memory.

Lisa could not understand why she had been experiencing a wave of anxiety for the past few weeks. Everything was going well in her life and she was looking forward to the free time she would have now that her five-year-old son would be going to school. She was even considering taking a part-time job. Tomorrow was to be Paul's first day of school and he was looking forward to it. Nevertheless, Lisa kept looking at him, searching for the hidden anxiety she assumed to be there. As she became aware of what was going on in her own head, she realized that her anxiety of the past weeks had been stirred up by her identification with her little boy. It was as though this were to be her first day of school, and she experienced herself once again as a little girl who had not wanted to be separated from her mother. She suspected that this had something to do with her procrastination in checking out job opportunities as well. Her present anxiety could be viewed as a feeling memory of the early situation with all of its conflict and anxiety.

There are similar types of feeling memory that come from the more remote past, from what Margaret Mahler calls "the bedrock of mental life that does not divulge its content and nature by verbal means—the 'unrememberable and the unforgettable.'"[1] These archaic memory-experiences are not usually based upon a single event but are built upon repetitive experiences whose fundamental quality permeated the early years of life. Because they are rooted in a time before there was language and thus before experience could be articulated and remembered as such, they seem to be totally irrational and even "crazy" when relived by persons who know themselves to be rational and competent adults. They may involve not only feelings such as anxiety or foreboding, but even unexplained perceptual shifts. I have known some individuals who, when these

1. M. S. Mahler, F. Pine and A. Bergman, *The Psychological Birth of the Human Infant* (New York: Basic Books, 1975), p. 197.

early memories were activated, experienced the room as becoming larger, much as it would have looked to them when they were very small.

Ginnie often experienced a vague apprehension that something she enjoyed would be taken away from her. The very fact that the fear was irrational upset her even more. Through therapy she was led to recognize clearly the frustration and despair she had experienced in infancy and childhood when she was not responded to in terms of her own needs and rhythms. Feeding, love and affection had been given her, but her parents had imposed upon her their own timetables and tastes. Often, for example, the nipple had been taken from her mouth while she was still hungry and needing to suck. This pattern based on the parents' wishes continued throughout Ginnie's growing years; and what went on in her interaction with her parents seemed to have little or nothing to do with her own state of being. She and her environment were always "out of sync."

When, in therapy, Ginnie's vague apprehension could be related to her earliest experiences of this nature it became possible to tease it apart from the reality of her adult experience and understand it in terms of its origin. Ginnie could have compassion for the little girl she once was and for the child's way of coping by attempting to comply and to please. She could understand that what seemed to be her irrationality made great sense in the light of her own history.

As I have said before, understanding how we got to be the way we are will not automatically make things better. It can provide foundation and direction, but if we are to truly grow and change we must commit ourselves to the process with all its inherent dangers. We must struggle against our own archaic paranoia, our sadism, our drive for vengeance, and our wish to retreat to the safety of mother's arms. At the same time we must make an effort to renounce the magic of our fantasied omnipotence and face the fact that we are merely human.

In the next chapters we will look back at the path we have all traveled since birth, particularly that of the first three years of life. This is the period when what Margaret Mahler calls the "psychological birth" of the human infant takes place. It is during these early years that a healthy and secure sense of self, the capacity to be, is consolidated. At the same time, the ability to relate to others as the real persons they are comes about. No longer are they valued simply because they meet one's need to be noticed or to be taken care of, or one's need for approval or validation. Thus loving develops hand in hand with being.

CHAPTER 4

BECOMING ONE:
THE BASIS FOR LOVING

Two souls with but a single thought,
Two hearts that beat as one.

VON MUNCH BELLINGHAUSEN

THE POET'S VISION of love as blissful union expresses the romantic dream of countless men and women. Plato wrote of the love between a man and a woman as a "meeting and melting into one another . . . becoming one instead of two. . . ." He explained this experience as an expression of an "ancient need . . . of something else which the soul of either evidently desires but cannot tell, of which (they have) only a dark and doubtful presentiment. . . ."[1]

What is this "ancient need"? What is the almost universal experience that lies at the core of this "dark and doubtful presentiment"? And why does awareness of a fantasy or wish for emotional union with another human being stir up fear and anger in the hearts of some instead of yearning and anticipation?

Without benefit of modern theories of child development, Plato intuited the early psychological unity of infant and mother which is subsequently lost and forgotten in the course of normal development. He sensed its relationship to the yearning of the adult for love as well. Unfortunately for some men and women this "ancient need"

1. Plato, *Symposium*, Great Books of the Western World, vol. 7 (Chicago: Encyclopaedia Britannica, 1952), p. 158.

41

presents a threat to hard-won individuality and cannot be allowed into conscious experience.

We are not born with the capacity to love, only with the potential for it.[2] Back at the very start of life there is no recognition of either self or other, no concern with conflicts between being and loving. Life is a series of fragments of bodily and sensory-motor experiences yet to be woven into meaningful patterns.

By the time the infant is four to five months of age, however, one notices a special smile and a general state of excitement and pleasure in response to the mother, or the main caretaking person. A special relationship, the *primary attachment bond,*[3] has been formed with her, and it is within the context of this relationship that the child will organize his or her fragments of experience into patterns which eventually will include other people and feelings about them. This special relationship, or primary attachment bond, thus plays an important role in the mental life of the developing infant. It constitutes the foundation of the capacity to love and also marks the point of departure from which the emergence of the self as separate from mother will soon take place.

THE ATTACHMENT PROCESS AND THE CAPACITY TO LOVE

The attachment process, which entails the participation and contribution of both mother and child, starts on the first day of life. A newborn child can be observed scanning the face of the caretaking adult and finally fixing on the adult's eyes. This eye-to-eye contact is the beginning of the ongoing psychological dialogue between mother and child which will eventuate in a special bond between them. René Spitz refers to this mother-child interaction as "mutual

2. Martin S. Bergmann, "Psychoanalytic Observations on the Capacity to Love," in J. McDevitt and C. Settlage, eds., *Separation-Individuation: Essays in Honor of Margaret S. Mahler* (New York: International Universities Press, 1971), pp. 15–40.
3. John Bowlby, *Attachment and Loss* (New York: Basic Books, 1969), Vol. I, p. 177.

cuing."[4] At any rate, many mothers naturally respond to the infant's search for eye contact by looking back and talking or making cooing sounds, thus reinforcing the child's innate attachment behavior. Other mothers may respond less readily and talk on the phone or read while feeding the baby. When this occurs often, even a breast-fed baby can be deprived of the dialogue which builds attachment and, eventually, the capacity to love.

The inherent nature of attachment-seeking behavior and the consequences of the failure of the environment to support formation of the bond are elucidated by research and clinical evidence from both animal young and human children.

Harry Harlow's experiments in the 1950s and 1960s[5] demonstrated not only that attachment-seeking behavior is innate in the baby rhesus monkey, but that the interaction between mother and infant is essential to the baby's capacity to relate normally to its own species. In Harlow's experiments, a variety of mechanical substitutes for real mothers were provided the baby monkeys. Some were made of wire mesh, some of terry cloth; some were warm and some were not; some had bottles attached for "nursing" while others had none.

Although the ability of the artificial mothers to give food via the bottles was obviously essential for the survival of the babies at one level, feeding alone was not enough to calm them when they were under stress. Under these circumstances they would cling to the terry-cloth mothers. At first the preference for the terry-cloth figures as soothers suggested that contact comfort was the essential psychological ingredient rather than being fed. But even with feeding and contact comfort these monkeys did not develop normally. Maternal response and the moment-to-moment interactions of considerable social complexity which go on between a live mother and her infant were found to be the *sine qua non* for normal development. When these deprived monkeys grew up, maternal behaviors were impaired. They were devoid of the capacity to care for or about

4. René Spitz, *The First Year of Life* (New York: International Universities Press, 1965).
5. Harry Harlow, "Early Social Deprivation and Later Behavior in the Monkey," in A. Abrams, H. H. Garner, and J. E. P. Toman, eds., *Unfinished Tasks in the Behavioral Sciences* (Baltimore: Williams and Wilkins, 1964), pp. 154–73.

their own babies. In fact, they were sometimes so abusive of them that the second generation of infants had to be separated from their real mothers for their own protection. Unloved babies could not grow up to be loving mothers. There is reason to believe that the same principle holds for human mothers.

STABILITY OF THE CARETAKING ENVIRONMENT

Observations of human children who have been placed in institutions during the first four years of life have also shed light on the importance of the early attachment bond with respect to the capacity to form lasting relationships. Children who had the opportunity to form an attachment before being placed did better, even though they experienced severe distress at the loss of the relationship, than did children who made no attachments at all. The effects of separation after the attachment bond has formed depend on a number of other factors, such as the quality of the relationship with the attachment figure before separation, and the quality of the environment and availability of new attachment figures after separation.[6]

Children reared in institutions are often cared for by many different people. One immediate result of this may be the decrease in visual responsiveness by the second month of life in infants reared in institutions and deprived of the maternal reinforcement of eye contact described in the previous section of this chapter.[7] At any rate, children raised in institutions are often described as clinging and dependent, and then attention-seeking and indiscriminate with respect to whom they turn to. In other words, they will be friendly to anyone who will respond to them. Subsequent studies of these children suggest that if they have *never* formed an attachment in the first two or three years of life, it is highly unlikely that they will do so

6. Michael Rutter, *The Qualities of Mothering: Maternal Deprivation Reassessed* (New York: Aronson, 1974).

7. R. L. Fantz, "The Crucial Early Influence: Mother Love or Environmental Stimulation?" *American Journal of Orthopsychiatry* 36, no. 2 (1966): 330–31.

after that time. In general they will relate to others chiefly to the degree that the other meets some immediate need.

Individuals who want to adopt a child who has had this kind of unfortunate beginning should be ready to understand and accept the child's impaired capacity to love. Their motivation should not be based on a fantasy or wish for a child to love *them*. If it is, inherent difficulties may generate not only disappointment but undeserved anger toward the child who does not respond in the manner expected. Only if they appreciate the hurt the child has suffered and its long-range consequences will adoptive parents succeed in bringing out the best in their son or daughter.

MOTHERING AND ATTACHMENT

In the earliest months of the child's life there must be, on the part of the mother, intense psychological involvement with her infant if she is to promote formation of the attachment bond. In this period of what D. W. Winnicott calls "primary maternal preoccupation,"[8] the mother must be in harmony with her baby's rhythms, emotions and physiological state. She must respond empathetically to what comes from the child, be it a cry or a smile. This focused attention and readiness to respond to the cues of the infant is referred to by Winnicott as a time-limited attitude. By this he means that it is appropriate only to this stage of the child's development.

When he or she is about four or five months old, the baby has formed the primary attachment bond and reached the stage referred to by psychologists as that of normal symbiosis. At this stage mother and self are experienced as a single unit. There is no differentiation between "me" and "you"; only the single pattern, "me-you." This stage of oneness is the basis of what Plato referred to as that ancient need of which we all can have only a dark and doubtful presentiment.

To understand this concept of psychological symbiosis, consider the analogy of the air you breathe. The air comes to you from the

8. D. W. Winnicott, "Primary Maternal Preoccupation," in D. W. Winnicott, *Through Paediatrics to Psycho-Analysis* (New York: Basic Books, 1975), pp. 300–305.

outside, yet it is experienced as part of you once you have breathed it in. Stop breathing for a moment, however, and you will become acutely aware of the reality that the air is *not* a part of you at all, but is something quite separate. You may, with practice, be able to hold your breath longer and make physiological use of the air already in your lungs—but only for a limited time. Sooner or later you must take in more air or you will die.

Just as prolonged absence of new air is likely to induce panic in you, so excessive and prolonged disruption of the connection with mother once the attachment has taken place will induce excessive anxiety in the baby. For at this stage of symbiosis, the mothering-person-experience is felt to be part and parcel of the self-experience. When the first is disrupted, so is the second, and the child experiences a general disorganization and anxiety. Too many such experiences run counter to the healthy buildup of a continuing sense of self and of the capacity to relate to others. The infant does not yet have the mental tools to deal with the disruption, and he may become overwhelmed by high levels of anxiety, rage, and depression.

If these feelings dominate the child's experience, they become incorporated into his view of himself and the world. As an adult, such an individual may still crave and be dependent upon human contact in order to counteract the distress felt at the disruption in this early stage. Other children with the same history may cope with the distress by becoming absorbed in the self. As adults they may seem to be unusually self-sufficient men or women. Often they have no feelings for others or live as loners.

The persistence of the drive for attachment and the strength of the bond once it has been formed are underlined by the fact that parenting does not have to be good for the process to take place. Indeed children also form bonds to abusive and/or ungratifying mothers, and strongly resist being separated from them.

THE UNSATISFACTORY SYMBIOSIS

When an adult seems to cling to an abusive or ungratifying relationship, it may seem evident to everyone else that he or she would be much better off without it. What friends and advisers fail to appreciate is the force of the pull toward just such a situation. If we dig a little deeper we are likely to discover that it is a kind of reenactment of the relationship with the early attachment figures as the individual experienced and interpreted it through the mind of the child. The individual has constructed the reality of today in a manner that is consistent with reality as it was experienced and understood long ago. Through an unconscious selection process in establishing intimate relationships the individual may ferret out qualities in the other person which make her or him a natural for the role of the early attachment figure with all the attendant demands, expectations, and reactions that characterized the childhood situation. In other cases these qualities are projected onto others in a more unrealistic manner with the result that the individual is likely to become involved in frequent conflict with persons who react with anger to being seen inaccurately or inappropriately.

There are also situations in which the attachment process does not go well because of seriously inconsistent patterns of caretaking. The child may live in his or her own home with his or her own mother but be assigned to the care of constantly changing maids and housekeepers. The discontinuity of experience interferes with the organizing process, and the child is in a chronic state of anxiety and anger. The mother's input is diluted, inconsistent, and generally unsatisfactory; but the continuing nature of her input does provide minimal structure. However, this inner structure is inadequate for future development and is clung to as an important basis for the child's sense of organization of self.

One woman of thirty-five with such a history could not accept the limits of what her mother could realistically give her. To do so would imply recognition that mother was a separate person rather than still some undifferentiated part of herself. She reacted with rage and fear at any suggestion that she diminish the intensity of her relationship with her mother because she was convinced that if she were to do so, she would die psychologically. In other words, she felt that her sense of self was so enmeshed with her image of her mother that extricating herself from the relationship would tear her apart in some way. When others pushed her in that direction, she experienced their efforts as a wish to destroy her. Sometimes it is difficult for people who are trying to help such an individual to understand why that man or woman becomes so enraged with them. He or she continues to struggle unsuccessfully to master the aborting and distorting of the love process at its inception, hoping to bring about the conditions that would have allowed it to evolve as it should have. Unfortunately, one cannot turn back the clock, and what would have been appropriate for a baby is not appropriate for an adult. Such a person is defeated time and time again, not only by the reality of the situation, but by the deep-seated fear and anger that will not go away.

In addition to the primary attachment bond formed with the mothering person, children normally make secondary bonds with other people in their world, such as the father, siblings, grandparents, or a regular baby-sitter. While the primary bond serves a vital organizing function, the secondary bonds help the child move away from the mother to become separate when the time comes. They counteract the excessive closeness that may develop when there is only the one attachment.

Secondary bonds can work against the formation of the single primary attachment bond if the mother does not have the interest in giving herself to that process. When this is the case multiple bonds may form, but no one relationship will be available for the construction of a unified me-you image. This may contribute to difficulty in intimate relationships later on.

Melanie tended to be overly sensitive to and upset by changes in other people, whether the changes were of mood or appearance. Any change, she felt, was tantamount to that person's becoming someone else. Somehow the threat of abandonment was associated with these experiences. The known person, in effect, left and was replaced by someone else, even though both were, in actuality, the same person. A common image in her fantasies and dreams was that of a five-headed monster.

In the first two years of life Melanie had been cared for not only by her mother, but by her grandmother and several aunts, all of whom lived together. Although the child was loved, there was an inconstancy to her day-to-day experience, with different faces, different hands, different styles of talking and handling. The nature of these caretaking experiences militated against the formation of the primary me-you image of symbiosis. Melanie dealt with the stress of the changing mothers and the unpredictability of experience by withdrawal to a space within herself where she wouldn't have to cope with the anxiety of the five-headed mother figure. As an adult she also used withdrawal to deal with the stress of too much social stimulation which seemed to pull her in many different directions. But then, although she would feel more unified, she would also feel empty and depressed.

If Melanie's mother had evidenced that "primary maternal preoccupation" that I mentioned earlier she would have provided the consistent mothering that her baby needed to form the bond that would constitute the basis for the capacity to love. As it was, her mother, self-involved and often depressed, left the care of her little girl to whichever of the other women was available at the moment.

In her analysis, Melanie was able to use her relationship with her therapist to bring the five-headed image together and to experience herself and others in a more cohesive fashion.

THE FALSE SELF

Another common problem which may originate during the attachment process and the stage of normal symbiosis is that of the false self.[9] A man or woman who feels real knows not only what he or she feels, but has access to other aspects of experience as well. Such an individual knows what he thinks, what he wants, what he perceives. Some people do not feel real. They describe themselves as feeling fraudulent, not knowing what they feel, think, want, or believe. They complain of lack of spontaneity, no pleasure in what they do or achieve, no sense of really being alive. Although they may seem to fare in superior style in the world, from their point of view none of it has any meaning for them. Upon close scrutiny, one can

9. D. W. Winnicott, *The Maturational Processes and the Facilitating Environment* (New York: International Universities Press, 1965), p. 152.

see that they live their lives as reactors rather than as initiators. Their entire identity seems to be carved out of adapting to their external reality. There is little awareness of anything inside.

The false self-identity is that of a reactive self—a self which takes its cue from the other—a responder but never an initiator. One can react by complying *with*, by struggling *against*, by performing *for*, by warding *off*, by complaining *about*. Reactive relating in the first years of life is not conducive to the development of the capacity to love, for loving can only be an experience of a real self. As an adult such an individual continues to relate to others through the false self-identity.

This situation comes about as the result of the inability or insensitivity of the mother who disregards or overrides the reality of what is going on with the child himself. When this happens her caretaking becomes an intrusion, an impingement—even an assault. A bottle stuck into the mouth of a screaming baby whose cries indicate a need for quieting and soothing is an attack upon the baby from his point of view. He may suck for a moment or two on the basis of reflex reaction, but then will take up his screaming once again. When this kind of interaction is characteristic of their day-to-day experience, the child's developing sense of self and other, the me-you pattern, becomes consolidated around its reactions to these impingements. The pattern becomes "reacting me/impinging you."

In healthy development the real self, the core self which is rooted in the child's own intrinsic bodily and sensory experience becomes connected to external reality through the mother as intermediary. When she fails in this function, the real self is isolated and shut out from the attachment relationship upon which the capacity to love is predicated. The dilemma of this child as an adult may be that the persistence of the yearning for intimacy exits side by side with the fundamental feeling, experience, and belief that one can only be real when one is alone.

Other men and women are even more cut off from their real experiencing self and are not able to recover it even in solitude. For even when they are alone, they continue to react to inner mental shoulds and demands just as they react to the shoulds and demands of others. Even in their fantasies they are reactors rather than originators. When they do form an apparently intimate relationship, it is often ridden with anxiety about doing the wrong thing. Despite periodic experiences of having their needs met which makes them feel good (reactively!), there can be no enduring loving connection as long as there is no real self available to it.

On the other hand, when the overall quality of mother-child interaction is based upon the mother's empathic response to what is initiated by the infant, the me-you pattern is based upon that which is intrinsic to the self, to the real core self.

THE CONFLICT BEGINS

In the second half of the first year of life, the child begins to become aware that he or she and mother are not one after all. He is on his way toward recognition that mother is a separate individual. It is at the point of transition, where experiences of "being one" alternate with experiences of "being two," that the conflict between loving and being comes to the fore.

Many adults still vacillate between the two states of experience that characterize this early stage. The pull of the yearning for the blissful union rhapsodized by poets is a threat to their sense of being, to their sense of self or identity. They express fears of disappearing or of being swallowed up. Yet staying separate confronts them with the anxiety of the loss of sense of connection, and they feel abandoned and depressed. They experience the full force of the conflict between being and loving.

Whatever the ancient need of which Plato wrote, the yearning for that blissful unity which foreshadows the capacity to love, there is another need which opposes it. This is the push toward individuation and the drive for autonomy which, very early in life, come to exist side by side with the pull toward the loved other. This process of separation and individuation[10] begins with the recognition that mother and self are, indeed, not one, but two differentiated entities. It is this recognition that constitutes the sense of "I am," that constitutes the capacity to be.

10. M. S. Mahler, *On Human Symbiosis and the Vicissitudes of Individuation* (New York: International Universities Press, 1968), p. 222.

CHAPTER 5

BECOMING TWO:
THE BASIS FOR BEING

THE SENSE OF ONE'S existence as a separate and real entity is the essence of "being." As I have already pointed out, the earliest awareness of a separate and real self comes about with the infant's recognition that he and mother are not a single unit after all. With this recognition that they have become two, the self is born.[1]

This gradual differentiation of "me" from "you" as well as of what is inside the self and what is outside it begins at about the age of five months and is the outcome of the infant's biological maturation. A particularly important factor here is the mental development that accompanies the growth of the child's brain and nervous system in general. The child becomes able to tell the difference between one person and another and gradually builds up a storehouse of memories.

Toward the end of the first year the infant's separation from mother is underlined by motor development. Increasingly, from the middle of the first year to the middle of the second, the child alternates moving away from mother with scurrying back to recon-

1. M. S. Mahler, F. Pine and A. Bergman, *The Psychological Birth of the Human Infant* (New York: Basic Books, 1975), p. 53.

nect with her once again. Margaret Mahler calls this scurrying back "emotional refueling." With the ability to crawl, and then to walk, the child can move away from mother under his own power. His sensory abilities and his capacity to extract meaning from what he experiences lead him to the recognition of "I am over here and she is over there."

Many adults, when pushed by well-meaning friends, guidance counselors, therapists, or simply by the demands of life to take on a measure of autonomy, are unable to do so. They have no sense of a separate and cohesive self, no clear feeling of "I am," upon which to build and to venture forth as independent men or women. Such individuals often number among the casualties of the encounter group for whom therapy aimed at facilitating independence has made things worse.[2]

As one young man who still chronically agonized with this dilemma put it, "If I move close I get lost, but if I move away I get lost." That is, if he moved closer to another person, he lost any sense of himself as separate; he lost the sense of "I am." If he moved away, on the other hand, there was no firm sense of self to sustain him.

This stage of becoming two is not without problems for both mother and child. One of these problems is separation anxiety which usually appears when the infant is eight or nine months old, although it has been observed earlier in some babies. At this stage the infant has two simultaneous and conflicting experiences to cope with: the experience of being one within the context of the symbiotic me-you pattern, and the experience of being two within the context of the increasing differentiation of self from non-self. With this dawning awareness comes the first conflict between being and loving, since this most primitive loving consists of being one with mother, while the most primitive being consists of being separate from her. At this point, however, there is still not a very clear-cut image of the self as distinct from the image of the mother. Paradoxi-

2. H. B. Roback and S. J. Abramowitz, "Deterioration Effects in Encounter Groups," *American Psychologist* 31, no. 3 (1976): 247–55.

emotional support that a mother gives to her young child. On the other hand, their self-esteem rides on their being competent and autonomous adults.

Fred is in this kind of no-win position. He feels neglected and angry if his dependency needs aren't met. And he feels resentful if they are met, since this undercuts his feelings of manhood. Just as the parent of the conflicted child finds it difficult to know how to respond to the mixed messages of the little girl or boy, so the adult partner of the man or woman who struggles with this conflict is likely to experience frustration, confusion, and helplessness. No matter how one responds, one will be met with anger or resentment.

I have encountered this pattern more in men than in women. This is not surprising inasmuch as the little boy is often pressured to be a little man who does not need Mommy's nurturing attentions, while the little girl is permitted this gratification. When this is true the boy cannot grow out of the conflict gradually, and thus never gets the chance to resolve it. As a grown man he is still caught between his repressed need for dependency and his need for self-esteem. Saying "no" is another way a child attempts to define himself as a separate person. It is a way of saying, "I am different from you." Some grown men and women still maintain a predominantly negativistic stance as a way to ensure their own boundaries of self. Their problem is not that they say yes when they want to say no but that they *must* say no even when they want to say yes. They need to preserve and protect the sense of self and this takes precedence over all other aspects of a relationship, including accepting affection.

Many young people and the adults they later become develop an entire identity based upon this kind of negativistic stance. They must reject everything that parents are and everything they stand for. When their own wishes and values correspond to those of their parents they must be denied. As I pointed out to one woman of thirty who was struggling with this issue, "You seem only to be able to define yourself in opposition to your mother." Her decisions, goals, attitudes, and opinions were determined by her need to do so; and because of this she was never truly free to explore and discover her

cally, although the growing sense of separateness is necessary for a sense of "I am," for being, separateness also is a threat to it.

As the sense of "I am" solidifies, the drive toward autonomy of the self becomes more intense. But the drive in turn creates anxiety as the child becomes more and more aware of the realities of his dependence upon his parents.

This conflict is especially intense in the second year of life; and it is often difficult for parents to understand why their child suddenly seems to be clinging and dependent at a time when increased mental and physical abilities should be making him just the opposite. One moment he will want to do things for himself; the next he will insist that someone do things for him.

The mother of two-year-old Douglas told me:

> "He wants to do everything himself. 'Douglas do it' is the catch cry for everything. This includes going to the fridge and getting himself a pickle from the jar, filling his own bottle, etc. Some things, like the latter, are simply impossible and denial often results in a lengthy tantrum. . . . He is *so* miserable, and even when he is screaming and stamping his feet, he's saying, 'Mummy' and 'uppie' between cries (although when I try to cuddle him he fights me). He really doesn't know what he wants. Eventually I calm him down and he has a bottle on my lap."

It is difficult for parents to know how to respond to these conflicting needs. Sometimes the parents' own confusion and frustration interfere with their being able to help their child. They have to promote and encourage autonomy, while providing the security that goes with having dependency needs met; and it is not easy to decide which to do when. As much as possible, helpful parents take their cues from the child. When the child is in the midst of the conflict, as was Douglas, there is little one can do other than weather the storm. Helping the child quiet down allows him to regroup his energies rather than being done in by the distress.

Sometimes adults, too, experience the same kind of conflict between their dependency needs and their drive for autonomy. On one hand they may seek a relationship which offers the kind of own nature. As Rollo May points out, this attitude interferes with the achievement of free will.

> ... protesting is partially constructive since it preserves some semblance of will by asserting it negatively. . . . But if will remains protest, it stays dependent on that which it is protesting against.[3]

Saying "no" is not enough.

And so, in the second year of life the conflict between the two antithetical drives, loving and being, is at its height. The pull toward mother with the need to stay emotionally connected with her is in opposition to the push away from her with its impetus to become a separate individual who can manage the challenges of life by himself or herself. It is a time of separation anxiety and of interpersonal strife which results from the need to oppose mother and all other adults as a way to affirm the self. This early conflict between the impetus toward separateness and the importance of the psychological bond, the uninterrupted sense of connection with mother, is experienced symbolically again and again throughout life. The entire life cycle is a more or less successful process of synthesizing the polarities of loving and being into a state of harmonious integration.

HOW PARENTS CAN HELP (OR HINDER)

The demand on the mother and on mother surrogates at this critical developmental crossroads is twofold: first, to continue to support the attachment bond by meeting the emotional needs of the child, and second, to promote and encourage the child's moves toward separateness.

As during the process of attachment, the mother will have to be able to support and nurture without feeling put upon or controlled by the infant's needs, and thus resentful of them. She will also have to

---

3. Rollo May, *Love and Will* (New York: Norton, 1969), p. 192.

possess a strong enough sense of herself as a person so that she will not want her baby to continue to need her in order to provide her with a role to play or to feed her self-esteem. Sometimes the child's attempts to define himself as a separate person stir up in the mother her own early anxiety over separation from her own mother, and she may react by becoming overprotective and blocking the child's moves away from her. If the mother experiences the child's moves toward separation as abandonment and punishes the child by withdrawing love or attention, the child is likely to experience his own abandonment fears. When this happens, the child is pulled between what are now experienced as mutually exclusive goals. Unable to integrate the drives toward loving and being, he may retreat from developing further in the direction of separateness and autonomy.

Whereas some mothers cannot tolerate the idea of their children growing up and not needing them, others are only too happy to be done with that burden of responsibility. Such a mother may resent the child's demands as intrusions upon her boundaries and autonomy and withdraw help and support before the child has developed psychologically to the point where this will not be experienced as abandonment. I have heard a number of men and women openly state that they refuse to grow up, because they are convinced that the price of growth is to be on one's own for all time with no right ever to ask or hope for help. They do not realize that a mature and autonomous adult can still say, "Hold me. Warm me. Comfort me." A child who is denied the continuing support he needs may develop pseudoindependence and maturity or, at the other extreme, cling to the unresponsive mother in fear or anger. As an adult, he will exhibit the same characteristics as he continues to struggle with the early dilemma.

Some parents fail to realize that their child is becoming a separate and unique individual. When this is the case, we find the parents reacting to the child as though he were an extension of themselves. They may expect him to walk sooner than the other babies on the block, to be an A student in school, to be socially popular, or to win the swimming trophy—or whatever—in order to serve their own pride and esteem. Often in this kind of family setup, the gratification of parental approval reinforces the child's readiness to relate in this manner.

A child who is expected to function as an extension of his parents can never develop a fully differentiated sense of self. Often as an adult he will establish relationships in which the partner communicates, as did his parents, "Stay here. I need you," or, "Go away. Don't bother me," or, "Be my gold star." In the first situation the partners become locked in by virtue of their mutual needs. In the second, a stance of pseudoindependence covers the long-split-off and repressed dependency needs, although the associated anxiety or depression may break through from time to time. And in the third situation, love and approval once again become contingent upon maintaining the partner's pride and self-esteem.

It is during the stage when the child begins to move away from the mother and into the world at large that the role of the father takes on greater importance. The secondary attachment bond which the child has made with him (as well as with other regular caretakers) makes the father a source of security which enables the child to increase his distance from mother without becoming unduly anxious. When there is no father, or when he is harsh or violent or cold and distant, the child's closeness with his mother is intensified. This makes it more difficult to develop as a person with a self that is separate from hers and more difficult to become independent of her later on when it is appropriate to do so.

Marriage is certainly no guarantee against the outcome described above, particularly when the father is unable or unwilling to parent his children appropriately and helpfully. Also there are many instances in which the mother actively shuts out the father because of her own needs for exclusivity in her relationship with her child.

Nevertheless new patterns of living, especially those of young women who elect to have and to rear children on their own certainly raise questions about the long-term effects of such arrangements. In many cases this mother-child dyad constitutes the entire interpersonal world of mother and child with the result that the mutual dependence for emotional nurturance is intense. Others who elect alternative styles of living do provide secondary attachment figures such as aunts and uncles or family friends who can serve the same function as the father in diluting the intensity of the developmental tie between mother and child.

Still, a child raised by his mother alone in an exclusive, intense relationship will have considerable difficulty in resolving the early dependent tie to her and in taking the necessary steps toward becoming two. Family therapy, the psychological treatment of an entire family together, often has as its goal the loosening of the tie and the structuring of the psychological boundary between mother and child.[4] The interest and cooperation of the father in this enterprise is essential to the process.

The consolidation of the sense of self, the experience and affirmation of one's being, is a long and complicated process which begins with the emergence of the self out of the symbiotic oneness with mother. It continues to be a lifelong concern for most of us.

Optimally it is a process which allows for the concomitant expression of love and intimacy. But the human experience is rarely optimal, and in the course of our psychological evolution we run head-on into a variety of problems and pitfalls. One of these is the issue of power which comes to the fore in the midst of the emergence of the self and recognition of mother as a separate entity. Children and the adults they become must eventually come to terms with what I call the power pivot.

4. Salvador Minuchin, *Families and Family Therapy* (Cambridge, Mass.: Harvard University Press, 1974).

6

THE POWER PIVOT

DEBORAH IS CAUGHT in a paradoxical bind which inevitably sabotages her relationships. Her self-esteem requires that she experience herself as perfect; and for her perfection means being all powerful. Imperfection is being without power or in someone else's power.

If Deborah finds herself attracted to a man who meets her standards and whose apparent power makes him especially desirable, her hopes for an idealized relationship are aroused. But—and here is the rub—if he is also attracted to her and wishes to pursue the relationship, there is a power shift. By virtue of his wanting her, Deborah now has power over him. This, as far as she is concerned, renders him imperfect and no longer desirable; in fact, she views him with contempt. At this point, of course, she no longer wants to see him. If, on the other hand, he is essentially indifferent and only throws her an occasional crumb of affection or attention, he remains powerful and therefore perfect. But Deborah then has to contend with the hurt of rejection. As a result she experiences her own powerlessness and imperfection. She is in a no-win position.

Deborah's problems with power and perfection can be traced back to the normal developmental process of becoming two during which these issues emerge. Up to then the child has participated in his mother's power and ability as part of her. As the sense of self evolves, however, the child is confronted more and more with the reality of his helplessness and relative inadequacy. There is a shift from the omnipotent self as part-of-mother to the powerless self who is a separate entity. Because of the central role this shift plays in the development of personality, it can be legitimately called the power pivot. The evolution of this shift is characterized by varying degrees of self-centeredness, a period of normal narcissism which, as Heinz Kohut points out, has important implications for later life.[1]

Resolution of the developmental stage of narcissism is essential to the capacity to love another person as himself or herself rather than as an object to meet one's narcissistic needs. If the child gets stuck at the power pivot, issues of power become central in later relationships, and love comes to be viewed as a fiction that people talk about but never experience. Situations of helping, giving, or caring take on overtones of demanding and submitting. As in Deborah's case, we find the individual rejecting all the pleasures of love out of hand. Healthy resolution of these issues enables the individual to develop the capacity to love a real and fully separate person and to construct a realistic image of himself.

Since the attitudes, expectations or ways of experiencing the self during the period of normal narcissism, or power pivot, so strongly influence an adult's self-image and relationships, it behooves us to consider the specific series of steps which comprise this period.

YOU ARE MY RIGHT HAND

When the process of becoming two is barely under way, physical separateness is recognized, but awareness of psychological separateness is a long way off. The child experiences and expects total power.

---

1. Dr. Heinz Kohut describes how some people maintain an illusion of their own grandiosity, or else how they may tend, instead, to overidealize and depend upon the other person. When the other fails to live up to the idealization (which he or she must, sooner or later), the individual reacts with anger and contempt and goes back to relying upon the overidealized self once again. *The Analysis of the Self* (New York: International Universities Press, 1971).

Mother is perceived as an extension of the self to be moved and controlled as one would move or control one's own arm or hand. Baby grunts and squeals, pointing to what he wants, and Mama gets it. Some children persist in this kind of behavior long after they have language for asking and long after they can get things for themselves. Often adults who relate to others in this way are given to rages or to sullen, angry withdrawals when their omnipotence is threatened. Generally, however, adults in whom the expectation of total power persists express it much more subtly. Others are expected to know what one wants and to provide it *without being asked*. When that fails to happen, the result may be angry silence or withdrawal. The other person's mind as well as his or her hand is expected to be an extension of one's own wish and will.

If such men or women do go into psychotherapy, they are usually unable to make use of it to grow. They enter the situation, primarily to find someone who will make them feel good by endlessly catering to their narcissistic demands for instant warmth, instant love, or total license to do and say whatever they want. When they discover that these responses cannot be coerced from the therapist they inevitably react with rage. Some even provoke the therapist into throwing them out, thereby proving their underlying thesis that people are no damned good. Others simply leave at the height of their rage to find someone else who will better fit their bill of particulars. They do the same thing in their private lives and have a life history of failed relationships, starting with the peer group of childhood on up to their adult years.

YOU ARE A REFLECTION OF ME

As the process of differentiation moves along, the child is confronted with new concerns. After an initial period of elation at the wonderful, newfound power of standing and walking and discovering the world beyond mother's lap, there is a letdown. The child now experiences the anxiety of its relative helplessness and of the possibility of loss of the needed other.

There is still, however, an inability to understand that the other person has feelings, moods, tastes, or any psychological qualities that are different from those of the self. Self and other are assumed to be psychological twins.

The adult who has not been able to move past this stage of the power pivot may be able to get along tolerably well with a "yes, dear" partner, but not with someone who has any shred of individuality and the wish to express it. When the partner fails to agree totally with what one feels, thinks, or wants, he or she is met with a mixture of anger and/or contempt. There may be a disgusted, "You don't understand me!" Since the loss of power provokes unbearable anxiety and the loss of perfection unbearable shame, the main defense against this distress is to retreat to the earlier stage of total power and domination of the other.

Some years ago I was doing research on value orientation, using a test that consisted of a number of paragraphs describing different ways to live one's life. A well-educated man to whom I showed the test material absolutely refused to believe that there was such a thing as a value orientation which differed from his own. He did not say, "I don't agree with the others." He adamantly insisted that they *did not exist.*

One young woman explained her distaste for making love with a man on the basis of the physical differences between male and female. Because he was unlike her, she experienced him as some kind of alien creature. She could only relate physically to a body which mirrored her own.

For the man or woman who persists in this way of thinking and relating, the connection with the other person is maintained by sameness and threatened by recognition of difference. This attitude is projected onto children as well as spouses, lovers or friends. "You and I are alike," may be a valid statement of similarities in taste, style, values, interests, temperament, and so on. But it may be based on a denial of the actual qualities of the spouse or friend and projection of some aspect of one's self onto him or her. In this instance, any expression of his or her true self by the other person is experienced as either rejection or abandonment, or as evidence of gross inferiority (since the self, of course, is perfect). When, on the other hand, the other person accepts the statement of twinship, he or she is "loved" and given much approval.

GIVE ME YOUR POWER

As the child's intellect and capacity to understand develop still further, he or she is ultimately confronted with the harsh reality of the self's lack of power and perfection. At this point the child turns dependently toward the parents whom he now sees as all powerful and perfect. They also become models for him and he imitates them and begins to build identifications with them.

The child's own realistic limitations to power can be tolerated if the parents intervene with help when it is needed during this period. If, on the other hand, parents are insensitive or unresponsive to the child's need for help, their toddler is likely to experience the anxiety that accompanies feelings of helplessness. He may deal with this distress in a number of ways. One is to regress to a belief in his own illusory power. As an adult, this individual may show an exaggerated self-sufficiency which covers over the repressed dependency needs. Or he may seek to protect himself from this anxiety by avoiding stressful situations. The refusal to attempt anything which holds the potential for failure would be such a defense. There are many men and women who have opted for this solution. They try to avoid failure and the anxiety of reawakened feelings of helplessness by never trying anything new or different.

In addition to turning to the parents for the lost sense of power, the child at this stage of development becomes dependent upon them for his self-esteem. When the parents support and recognize the child's growing competence with "Good for you! You can do it," for example, they forge a link between the child's self-esteem and reality. In other words, the child's self-esteem connects with what he or she actually can do rather than with fantasy or delusion. Parents who overdo praise, however, with the mistaken notion that this is the way to build up the child's self-esteem, often fail to face the reality of the child's limited capabilities and his need for guidance and instruction. They reinforce the child's earlier gradiose beliefs about himself. In the adult this illusory grandiosity (usually secret) exists side by side with low self-esteem in realistic situations.

Men and women who do not have reality-based self-esteem may continue to need others as a source of good feelings about themselves as well as a source of feelings of power. The other is needed to counteract feelings of shame and helplessness.

We see this attitude in June, who derives her self-esteem vicariously through her husband's business successes. Reverses in her husband's business are likely to provoke in such a woman rage at his failure rather than support during the crisis. For by the act of failing, he has ceased to be that source of power and perfection upon which she depended.

Paradoxically, the individual who operates in this manner wants power over the needed other person who is then required to be all powerful and all perfect. This wish for control is often less conscious and less obvious than that of the person who considers the other to be an extension of the self. But it is there nonetheless. June is saying, "I need you to be powerful, to be perfect, and to be completely under my control so I can make sure of my own power, so I will never have to experience feeling weak, frightened, helpless, or humiliated."

The paradox—be all powerful but submit to my control—creates an unresolvable bind for the person who receives the contradictory messages. He or she is to both submit to being controlled and play the part of the all-powerful parent.

This scenario is often played out covertly through manipulation. In her book, *The Total Woman*,[2] Marabel Morgan outlines a way to achieve total domination over the husband through seduction. Her obvious contempt for the male comes through in her conscious manipulation of his little-boy needs to be praised and made to feel important. Once this has been achieved, the man will supposedly only want to be with his wife because she makes him feel good. He even will give up his association with friends to stay

2. Marabel Morgan, *The Total Woman* (New York: Simon and Schuster, Pocket Books, 1975).

home with her. She now has him secure within her silken net. Morgan is apparently totally unaware of the fact that a healthy man might react negatively to this kind of bondage. She would probably react with wide-eyed hurt and surprise at being told that she was being controlling. After all, he is the one with the power.

With all her protesting that she believes that women should submit to men, Morgan's message to women is one of power—how to get it and how to keep it.

Sometimes the power issues of the human personality become institutionalized in the culture and politics of society. The attraction to charismatic and powerful leaders derives from the wish to share in their perceived power, and thus to feel less helpless and humiliated. In psychological terms this is called "identification with the aggressor." It is a phenomenon which is manifest in gangs, and in the slavish acceptance of whatever the gang leader proposes. The feelings of power and perfection that one derives from an idealized parent figure are also manifest in such social-cultural anomalies as est. Here we find the playing out of the final stage of the power pivot taking place not between one individual and another, but on the stage of a large meeting hall, where we are confronted with the aberration of a folie à dix milles.

Any man or woman who makes the other responsible for his or her self-esteem is caught at this point of the power pivot. Whether it is being paid attention to at a party, being responded to with adequate enthusiasm, or being called on Wednesday—when the other person has the power to bestow or take away self-esteem by his or her behavior we are endowing that person with the power and perfection that we once lost and still seek to reclaim.

THE ROLE OF PARENTS

Parents play a dual role in the facilitation of their child's successful negotiation of the power pivot. On one hand, their emotional availablity enables the seeds of love from the earlier stage of oneness with mother to grow and to flourish. Because there is a basis for love and trust which parents continue to enhance by their availability, the child is enabled to forego his need to dominate in order not to lose them. This is the critical point at which power over the other may come to substitute for love, the juncture at which power instead of love may become the dominant theme in an individual's life.

On the other hand, the healthy parent begins to make demands and have expectations that are *appropriate for the child's age and his or her ability to meet them*. These demands and expectations are an essential nudge, a push out of infantile omnipotence and egocentricity. They enable the child to begin to care for his own needs, to control his behavior and his impulses, and to realize that he will be expected to be aware of and respect the needs, feelings and boundaries of others. Without this nudge the child may fail to move toward independent functioning and self-regulation. Sometimes, because of her own need to keep the child dependent, her view of him as an extension of herself, or erroneous ideas about good mothering a mother fails to give this necessary push and, in fact, rewards and reinforces the child's omnipotence-laden attitudes. If, for example, the mother fails to correct her child's delusions of power and perfection and persists in responding to him as though he were the center of the universe, the child will grow up expecting the world to cater to him in the same manner.

There is a growing incidence of such self-centered orientation in adults as well as their children; and, to a regrettable extent, it can be laid at the door of psychology books on childhood written by professionals a generation ago. Parents were made to feel that any frustration they caused their children would lead to neurotic conflict that would supposedly interfere with the children's happiness and creativity. They were taught quite directly that children were the most important people in the family and that the adults existed to give them what they wanted. The idea of the child-centered family even influenced design and architecture. Parents would not dream of taking a trip without the kiddies. And lest poor Johnny be upset when Billy got a present, Johnny got presents on Billy's birthday, and vice versa. Children were never to have to wait, to go without, or to be out of the spotlight of parental adulation and attention. The concept of meeting the child's needs was grotesquely misapplied, and the omnipotence and grandiosity of an entire generation were nurtured and reinforced to the point where they became central to their personalities later on.

It is also unfortunate that issues of power in human relationships, which have their genesis at the stage of the power pivot, have become politicized. It is unfortunate that the archaic angers of women have been mobilized in a manner which defines the man as "enemy," precluding the potential for resolution of these issues in a manner which still leaves room for negotiating a new and more mutually gratifying relationship.

When these early developmental issues can be extricated from the reality issues of economics and social status, women will be able to work more effectively in these important arenas. They will be able to mobilize their real competence and not need to relate to men in the old ways, but yet be able to relate as loving equals. One would hope that consciousness raising for both men and women would help people sort out love issues from power issues.

When both parties love themselves in the form of a healthy self-esteem rather than on the basis of grandiose illusions, and cherish the other as the real and whole person she or he is rather than as someone to meet needs of power and self-esteem, then power issues will not be there to interfere with loving.

Power tactics such as those proposed by the "total woman" will be renounced as the psychological whoring that they are, and loving partners will be able to give and take, help and be helped, take care of and be taken care of on the basis of the exigencies of the moment, each person comfortable in either role rather than being locked into one or the other by power issues left over from the second and third years of life and the critical stage of the power pivot.

It is only with the eventual renunciation of the fantasy of the idealized self or the idealized other, with the acceptance of one's realistic competence as opposed to fantasy omnipotence or impotence, and of one's real nature as some kind of mixture of good and bad as opposed to an illusion of perfection or worthlessness, that any of us can go forth as real men or real women to make a loving relationship with another real man or real woman.

Given human limitations, the built-in paradoxes of the developmental process, and less than optimal life circumstances, growing up is likely to leave each of us with unresolved problems of the psyche still to be dealt with in adult life. One of these is dependency, a state of being in which one continues to experience the other as a powerful parental figure, and which has troublesome consequences of its own.

CHAPTER 7

NEEDING AIN'T LOVING

IN THE PREVIOUS CHAPTERS we have seen that one of the most important aspects of the developmental stages of the first three years of life is dependency. In the preattachment period, the child depends upon others to care for his or her basic creature needs and to keep alive. During the stage of symbiosis, the child also depends upon the mother to help him make sense out of the world and his experiences in it. With the process of becoming two, the process of separation and individuation, the child depends upon others to help him further develop a sense of self by validating and affirming it. Then, as the sense of self becomes more secure the child grows out of his dependency. However, each of the normal developmental manifestations of dependency often reverberates in adult life. That is, adults experience similar kinds of emotional needs although usually not as obviously, and although they may be otherwise self-sufficient men or women.

We are all dependent to some degree. The need for love, affection, friendship, and support are part of the human condition. Having a partner, playing together, loving together, being available to each other for comforting from time to time can make life less burdensome and contribute to a sense of well-being. But a healthy sense of self allows for many options with respect to life-style, be it with a partner, a family, or as one who elects to live alone. The individual who experiences the lack of a partner as a calamity to be avoided at all costs often has a dependency problem.

Labeling the dependent man or woman as childish, assuming that he or she is afraid of adult responsibility, obscures the concerns that lie below the fear. Indeed, many people who are tormented with this kind of anxiety, and who therefore cling to unsatisfactory relationships, carry a great deal of responsibility in their lives, particularly in their business or professional lives. They are obviously neither helpless nor inadequate men and women.

While some people renounce relationships and the wish for intimacy and attachment in order to protect and preserve their identities, their "right" to be themselves, the overly dependent may opt for a quite different resolution of the conflict between being and loving. They often surrender their selfhood and pay a price in stunted growth, with a perennial struggle against anxiety, depression, and shame.

Exploring some of the various manifestations that problem-ridden dependency may take in adult life, one can see how they relate to the dependencies of early development. For instance, like the child of the stage of being one, an individual may need others to assure him that he exists. And like the child who experiences his separateness but feels small and helpless, others may be needed to make the self feel valued. It will be different for different people, depending upon their own unique developmental history.

I NEED YOU TO CONVINCE ME THAT I EXIST

Whenever someone Fran saw regularly in her office failed to acknowledge her with a smile or a hello, she would feel wiped out, as though she did not exist. Not only would she become anxious because of the shakiness of her sense of her own continued existence, but she would become furious at the other person whom she blamed for her discomfort. According to her way of thinking, that person had not only the power but the responsibility for validating her existence. She felt quite justified in her outrage at the other's failure to live up to this "responsibility."

Whatever the responsibility of the early mother to help organize and then to confirm her small child's sense of self, persons in one's adult world become resentful and justifiably angry at having this responsibility laid on them. An individual who, because of unfortunate or unsatisfactory early experiences, is stuck at this point, is in a quandary. On one hand he is dependent upon others for validation. But on the other hand, because of unrealistic and inappropriate expectations and demands, he brings upon himself anger, censure, and broken friendships instead. He is caught in a perpetual vicious cycle of intense need for others and angry disruptions of relationships which then intensify his need.

Often people caught in this dilemma withdraw and nurse a silent rage, which they communicate nonetheless. But sometimes they accommodate, adapt and behave in a placating manner in order to bring about the kind of response needed to alleviate their anxiety about their existence. In so doing, they give up and lose any sense of their own identity.

Often this need for validation shows itself in little ways and is played out covertly, without conscious recognition of the process. Sally and Jim are at a party. Sally tentatively comments on the play they saw the previous evening, all the while watching Jim's face. As she sees the tightening at the corners of his mouth that signals disapproval, both her voice and spirit fade away. The challenge to her right to an opinion of her own also challenges her very right to be, and she loses all sense of herself as a viable being. In a dependent relationship, when one relies upon the other to confirm, validate, or endorse the self, the self may be sacrificed to the requirements of the relationship, and thereby lost.

I NEED YOU TO TELL ME WHO I AM

Just as some people use others as a kind of mirror to reassure them that they exist, so others use the people upon whom they depend as a mirror to define them, to tell them who they are.

An example of this is the living of one's life and the experiencing of one's self through a given role. This is, by and large, a most common and widespread way of living life. Roles, whatever they may be, offer a kind of security and predictability. Yet, by its very nature, role playing and role living can only be at the expense of authentic being and genuine loving.

When one lives his life and experiences himself through a role, he needs others because of their function in a cast of characters that is essential to his own particular role, be it that of parent, child, strong one, or sick one. A child needs a parent if he is to be a child. A strong one needs a weak one, and a sick one needs a caretaking one.

Narcissistic mothers who are insensitive to the needs of their infants may create sons and daughters who from early on learn to adapt to the psychological needs of the mother instead. The children become adept at sensing the mother's needs and lend themselves to roles required by the psychology of the family as a whole. The role of caretaker, of the child being parent to the parent, is not at all unusual. As adults, such children continue to relate through the caretaker role, be it with friends, spouses, or children. They find it difficult if not impossible to relate on any other basis.

Jonathan was such a child. When he was nine years old his father died and his mother went into a depression from which she never recovered. As the older child, Jonathan felt the responsibility for his little sister. Furthermore, he realized he would have to take care of his mother, too, to help her function as a parent so she could take care of him in turn. As a way of coping with his anxiety at the possibility of total abandonment, he became parent to his parent.

When I met Jonathan, he was an exhausted and driven man who was caring for a chronically depressed wife and for his children whom he infantilized and overprotected. He complained a great deal that no one seemed to care at all about his needs.

But Jonathan was unable to let himself be tended to even if someone did want to respond to him in this manner. His self-esteem had become tied up with his being able to play the caretaker role. Furthermore, giving it up carried the threat of feelings of shame and failure, and would have confronted him with his childhood feelings of helplessness—feelings which were now consciously experienced as self-doubt and a sense of unworthiness.

This kind of covert dependency played out through role relating requires a reciprocal stance on the part of the partner. If the wife is the strong one, the husband must be the weak one, at least on the surface of things, and vice versa.

In some marriages the man maintains his role of the strong one by keeping a tight control of the purse strings so that his wife must come to him for money much as a child must go to a parent. Should he lavish gifts on his wife, he still plays the role of parent, albeit an indulgent one. In this sort of marital relationship, wishes or attempts on the part of the wife to work and make money of her own will be negated with a pseudoprotective, "I don't want *my* wife to work," or by an active undermining of her confidence in her ability to do so. While the man is defined as the strong one, hiding his dependency, the woman is defined as the weak one, hiding the strengths which would jeopardize her husband's self-esteem. But the wife's dependency needs are operating in this situation as well. She participates in the arrangement because her needs would be endangered by her husband's anger should his needs not be met.

This sort of arrangement founders when one of the partners wearies of his or her role and begins to press for change. The strong one may grow tired and resentful of the burden. A giving one may come to feel depleted and deprived. The self-esteem of the needy one surfaces in angry protest, and both partners begin to wonder if the dependent attachment which they have been calling love is worthy of the surrender of their authentic being.

The problem of covert dependency in women is far less common because there are social rewards for them in taking a dependent stance in life. In fact, a woman is likely to meet with hostility and ridicule if she shows too much strength—whatever "too much strength" might be. She may be deemed "castrating" or "unfeminine," both of which are sufficiently abhorrent to her to inhibit her assertive or independent behavior.

Some years ago Denise found herself on a hike through the woods with a group of men and women. She had scrambled up a rather steep hill and looked back to see her husband, a large, heavyset man having difficulty negotiating the climb behind her. She automatically reached out and offered him her hand. He took it and, regaining his footing, reached the top of the hill. It was very soon evident that he was angry with her, feeling she had robbed him of his (precarious) manhood.

A short time later Denise found herself playing an old game familiar to women, especially to able and competent women. She pretended to need his help when, indeed, she did not, in order to help him regain his lost self-esteem as well as not to have him be angry with her anymore. But by the end of the day, with feelings of dismay and disgust, she had become aware of the enormity of the charade, and of its cost in terms of her own sense of integrity and being.

This was one of those turning points when a decision is made that alters for all time the course of one's life. Denise would no longer play the role of the helpless and dependent one in the interest of maintaining someone else's self-esteem. If there were to be a relationship, the other person would have to accept her with all her strengths and weaknesses. It was one of many decisions and changes which put more and more stress on a marital bond that would eventually give way under it. In essence, she had decided not to sacrifice her being so that she could have loving.

Just as some role relationships are based upon strength and weakness, others are based on giving and taking. In healthy, nondependent, mutual relationships, giving and taking are part of the natural flow and rhythms of the relationship. There is no rigid role assignment. Caring unites with sensitivity, and each participant in the relationship can find a way to be in harmony with his or her own being as well as with that of the other. Being is not in conflict with loving.

I NEED YOU TO KEEP ME FROM FEELING LOST

In addition to role playing, other people can be used to serve the function of a center for the organization of one's world, simply by virtue of being there. This derives from the early mother's organizing function for her child. This is first manifest in the me-you image of the stage of being one. Later, as the child becomes more separate, mother, father, and home become the center of security and familiarity in the child's life.

For a small child, one of the most difficult aspects of loss through death or separation from a parent is the fact that suddenly the world is a different place. Reality itself has changed. This is one of the reasons why, when the mother must be away (as in the hospital with a new baby), keeping the child's world as normal as possible reduces the severity of psychological stress. The more strange and alien elements there are in it for him, the more painful and frightening the separation from mother will be.

To some extent, abrupt and extensive changes in the life of adults, changes which separate them from those on whom they are dependent, may evoke an uncomfortable separation anxiety. The security of the self is still tied to the physical presence of the other.

At a university far from home, Karen wrote to me. "It's hitting me real hard how alone I am down here, and I'm scared. . . . There is no going back, that I realized tonight also, and I sit here crying as I understand that I am so afraid to go forward, but have no choice." She went on: "I want to call Steve back and beg for the relationship we once had. I want to call up my parents and tell them I'm coming home." And then she said, "I hear you in my mind saying many times to me, 'Don't go out and get hooked up with someone right away. Be alone for awhile.'" She struggled with "trying to convince myself that I am indeed a whole person who can pull through hard times and go through changes and be loved and love again."

The more one has to depend upon external persons or situations to help feel securely anchored in life, the more intense the anxiety of separation from the needed others will be. The more one depends upon others for his sense of identity, for his self-esteem and self-confidence, and for his sense of security in the world at large, the more he will have to cling to old relationships or to form new ones which serve the same function for him.

I NEED YOU TO MAKE ME FEEL PERFECT

Certain kinds of dependent relationships are used to maintain the illusion of the perfect, idealized self that normally is lost during the developmental stage of becoming two. In one instance, the illusion of one's perfection is maintained by assigning a negative aspect of the self to a spouse, a child, or even a friend through a technique referred to as projective identification. For instance, some children are depended upon to play out negative aspects of their parents' selves so that the latter can feel super-adequate. Parents of such children may actually manage to produce a son or daughter who, despite good native intelligence, plays out the stupid and inadequate role. This attitude preserves the attachment to the needed parent. It also functions more covertly as a way to get even for the humiliation that goes with the role. The child "forgets," makes mistakes, wets the bed, breaks and spills, and gets away with hostile behavior on the basis of the shared myth of his inadequacy. "He can't help it. . . . he's just not well coordinated." Parents often overtly deplore the handicap; but at the same time they continue to foster it by endless helping, advising, and overall infantilizing of the needed partner. If they take the child to a therapist, they actively sabotage any efforts to change the situation.

Because both partners in this kind of relationship lack an integrated self, they cannot function independently of their psychological collaborator. Such relationships, often between grown men and women and their elderly parents as well as between spouses, are intense, involved, and apparently insoluble. The attachment takes precedence over the integrity of the self, over being. The participants label it "love" but it has more to do with mutual interdependency than loving.

Sometimes a partner is needed to function as a supplement, as a replacement for a lost or split-off valued aspect of the self. The self is felt to be incomplete. The other is experienced as making the self whole once again.

Terry, afraid since early childhood to assert himself in any way lest he meet with his mother's cold and disapproving withdrawal, was powerfully drawn to highly assertive women. He saw them as having the "vitality" which he lacked. His fundamental sense of being alive was buried along with repressed anger toward his controlling mother who punished him for asserting himself against her control.

For a time, in his relationships with women Terry would feel, once again, whole, alive, and vital. He would "fall in love" with the needed partner. In effect what this meant was that he would relate to the woman as an extension of himself in order to participate in her vitality. In time the boundary between what was himself and what was the woman would get very fuzzy, and eventually he would lose the sense of himself as a separate person. When he struggled to regain this sense of being he would be left feeling depleted and powerless once again.

A person who uses another individual to complete his sense of self is in a state of constant dependency. The other person supplies what is missing, but he or she can also take it away! The self of the dependent person must be even further compromised so as not to alienate the essential partner who has been chosen as the bearer of the lost attribute.

I NEED YOU TO MAKE ME FEEL GOOD ABOUT BEING ME

As the child renounces his illusions of power and perfection, he depends upon the approval of parents to sustain his self-esteem. This form of dependency is also exhibited by many adults who are vulnerable to feelings of worthlessness and unlovability. Needing another person's approval in order to feel good about themselves, they may try to "psych out" the other person's wishes and behave accordingly, surrendering their own authenticity and spontaneity in the process.

Freedom from such extreme concern for pleasing other people is rooted in early experiences with a truly nurturant and accepting world. If positive parental responses are forthcoming only when the child feels, behaves, or thinks as parents deem he *should,* he will be unable to make their "Good for you!" reactions a part of himself because they will have nothing to do with how or who he *really* is. The praise will be for his pretense not his real, natural self which will remain unconfirmed. Living up to parental standards may be based on fear either of punishment or of losing approval of parents or of new people who have been given parental authority and power. Consequently, one's self-esteem is placed in the hands of others. To protect that self-esteem, one may strive to live up to the requirements of others at the cost of being in harmony with one's authentic self.

Healthy self-esteem means that an individual lives in accordance with the ideals, values, and moral and ethical standards that he himself has formulated as part of the process of psychological maturation.

One patient of mine was chronically anxious about how people would respond to her. She tried to be as good and as perfect as she knew how so that she would be liked by everyone. It wasn't working.

When I asked her what her favorite fruit was, she replied that it was the apricot. I asked her to pretend that she was an apricot—the most beautiful, perfectly ripe, unblemished apricot there ever was. Then I asked her to imagine someone coming along who did not like apricots and what that person's reaction to her would be. She made a sour face.

Then I asked her to pretend that she was another apricot—smaller, not so perfect, with a little bite taken out by a bird and a freckle on the other side. I asked her to imagine this time that someone came along who *loved* apricots. She smiled, understanding what I had been trying to tell her about being one's self and being loved.

No matter how hard we may try to please or to be good (whatever that is!), we surely cannot please everyone. This dooms any efforts at self-confirmation through the eyes of other people.

I NEED YOU TO MEASURE ME AGAINST

At the time of the power pivot, the child moves from the illusion of magical control over mother as an extension of the self, to recognition of the separateness and inadequacy of the self vis-à-vis a powerful parent. It is not until the child has developed further along and achieved a sense of his own realistic competence and image of the self and the other, that this, "I'm powerful, you're weak," or, "I'm weak, you are powerful," dichotomy can be resolved. Since power and self-esteem (versus powerlessness and shame) go together in the early years, other values which are later accepted as a measure of one's worth may fall into this same sort of mutually exclusive dichotomy when the early struggle remains unresolved. Although the struggle in adult life seems to be *against* the other, that person is needed to provide the self-defining contrast.

One young woman would say of her sister, "She's prettier, but I'm smarter." Her feelings about herself, about her attractiveness or lovability or capability, were not firmly anchored in herself but could only be grasped through a comparison with her sister and with others in her life as well. She needed her relationships as a kind of nucleus around which to organize her perception of herself.

Unfortunately, this kind of relating automatically introduces a hostile and competitive element into the basic dependency. In order to feel good about one's self, the other person has to be seen in a bad light. If one is up, the other must be down, and vice versa. We've probably all seen this kind of seesaw relationship and wondered why it continues in view of the degree of competitive hostility. It continues because each would feel lost without the other through whom the self can be compared, perceived, and defined.

HOSTILE DEPENDENCY: THE COMPROMISE THAT DOESN'T WORK

Fighting is one way to stay close and involved, to have one's various dependency needs met, and at the same time to protect the self by asserting its separateness. Dependent clinging and oppositional behavior often go hand in hand.

This mode of relating is normal behavior for the dependent two-year-old who is trying to establish a degree of autonomy, but it is the cause of serious problems in adult relationships. As a compromise solution to the conflict between being and loving, it just doesn't work. The hostility precludes the gratifications that go with closeness, while the dependency precludes the development of identity and the unfolding of the real self.

Tom was caught on the horns of this dilemma in his relationship with his wife. The need to oppose her in order to feel separate stood as a barrier to anything positive or affectionate that might take place between them. If his wife reached out warmly to him, the closeness that this implied was experienced as a threat to his autonomy. (Closeness with his mother had meant complying with her demands.) He would push his wife away, but then he would feel empty, futile, and depressed, at having to deny himself the love for which he yearned. He had to say no when he wanted to say yes.

The evolution of the hostile-dependent relationship is exemplified by a boy of ten who asked me to teach him to play the piano. I responded to his apparent eagerness to learn and bought a beginner's piano book for him. The first lesson involved learning the letter names of the keys. We began by finding middle C, and then all the other Cs. Lesson after lesson went on, and each time I would start by asking him to find all the Cs. One time he played all the Bs. The next time he played all the Ds. He was intelligent, but he seemed "unable" to master this simple assignment. One day he broke into a big grin, and I realized that he had something else in mind than learning to play the piano. I told him to let me know when he had mastered finding where all the Cs were, and then we would go on with our lessons.

It was clear that this little boy was interested, first, in involving me in a helping relationship, and then in thwarting my efforts to help him. A child who develops this kind of self-defeating behavior does not do so out of some perverse pleasure in failing. His defeat of parentified figures, however, does gratify his need for power over them and makes sure that they do not have any power over him. Most importantly, he protects the boundaries of his real but inadequately defined and frightened self. He forms dependent attachments such as that which he has with his mother, and at the same time maintains his separateness by opposing and thwarting those with whom he forms the relationships.

At school this kind of child is usually identified as an underachiever. He defeats his teachers by being inept or stupid. His inevitable failure wreaks havoc with his self-esteem despite the fact that he feels a sense of secret power at having defeated the parent figure.

If this chapter has seemed to be a chamber of horrors of love gone sour, they are everyday horrors that many, many men and women agonize over, rage against, or succumb to. Needing is not loving. It reflects the inability to love another person as a whole person in his or her own right and who is cherished for being that person. Needing also reflects the thwarting of being insofar as the self must be surrendered to the requirements of the relationship.

Acting out the patterns of needing unhappily perpetuates the very blocks to being and loving which they were devised to protect from or compensate for. They paradoxically bring about the death of relationships or the annihilation of individuality.

Resolution of the conflicts of the power pivot and moving beyond dependency bring the individual to a new and enviable level of relating. In the recognition and valuing of the real self and the real other lies the potential for mature loving which ultimately enhances one's capacity to be.

CHAPTER 8

THE BEST OF ALL POSSIBLE WORLDS: BEING ME AND LOVING YOU

As the young child moves forward out of the stage of the power pivot, idealistically he achieves a cohesive and realistic sense of self as well as a realistic sense of the other people in his world. As an adult he will be able to value persons on the basis of the persons they are rather than on the basis of what they can do for the self. Loving the other will be just as important as being loved *by* the other.

As this stage of development—that is, when the child is about three years old—he becomes better able to tolerate both good and bad feelings about himself as well as toward others. The capacity to tolerate ambivalence will make it possible later on to establish relationships which will endure in the face of disappointment and anger. And finally, at this stage the child consolidates the capacity to nourish, comfort, validate, and confirm himself from inner resources that will enable him, as an adult, to be alone or to live alone without being lonely, depressed, or afraid.

Developmental tasks which confront the individual at each of the successive stages throughout life—going off to school, adolescence, becoming an independent adult, middle age, and coming to terms with death—involve the same issues, although in ever more intricate and complex ways. But if the foundation has been well laid in the first three or four years of life, the later challenges can be met with a minimum of distress and a maximum of fulfillment.

BECOMING WHOLE

Intellectual maturation combines with satisfactory life experiences to promote a continuing process of integration. This includes the integration of perceiving, thinking, feeling, wishing, and doing—all different aspects of the experiencing self. Recognition and integration of these sometimes conflicting aspects of self are essential to the process of becoming whole. I may feel angry but wish I were not; I may believe a friend is loyal but perceive he is not; I may feel bored but choose not to show it in my behavior. All of these are elements of me, and I must be able to tolerate and resolve the conflict between them if I am to "be me."

The process of becoming whole also involves the healing of the good me/bad me split along with the good you/bad you split. This is a normal developmental split which originates in the stage of symbiosis when positive experiences are grouped together in the good me-you image, and negative experiences are grouped together in the bad me-you image. Gradually, in the stage of becoming two, the me

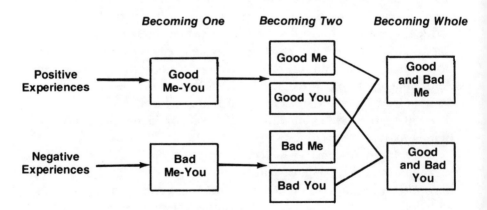

is differentiated from the you. Now, the split halves of the me image and the you image must be integrated into single, unified images of a whole self and a whole other.

The continued split of others into either all good or all bad images, and with this, the inability to tolerate ambivalence, is a major factor in the breakdown of relationships. When there are disappointment and anger, the good one becomes the bad one, and in so doing, ceases to exist. The emotional connection with the loved one is lost, and what is felt instead is the unmodified hate toward the bad one.

The untempered hate for the all-bad self can be just as toxic. It can destroy the connection with the valued self and wipe out self-esteem. In the most extreme instances, such rage and hatred may find expression in actual killing, that is, in murder or suicide.

When the final step of integration is successful, the capacity to tolerate an attitude of ambivalence replaces feelings of total, idealized love or total hate. People—including one's self—are experienced as neither devils nor saints, but as the real persons they happen to be. This is a basic requirement for being me and loving you.

The process of becoming whole also entails the healing of the split which derives from the power pivot. The integration of feelings of omnipotence with feelings of helplessness, and of belief in one's perfection with feelings of worthlessness and shame accompany an increasingly realistic view of parent figures. They are no longer viewed either as under the power and domination of the self, or as the source of all power.

This final step toward being me and loving you is a complex operation that is subject to influences from the preceding stages of development. The attitude of basic trust toward the world, which is set up in the first year of life, gives the child the courage to renounce the illusion of power. With the continued emotional availability of parents during the stage of becoming two, the child's awareness of his realistic helplessness and imperfection, with accompanying feelings of anxiety and shame, are counteracted by the parents' support and acceptance. Emotional support of this nature enables the child to relinquish the need for power and the illusion of perfection. It makes it possible for him to take the final step away from the power pivot toward authentic being and authentic loving.

It is the same for all of us as adults. It is certainly easier to admit an error (and thus, imperfection) to someone who genuinely cares for and respects us. It is another matter to do so to someone whose feelings for us are less positive. In the first instance, one can be wrong without feeling shamed. And in such a relationship, one can truly be me and love you.

BEING ALONE WITHOUT BEING LONELY

An individual's capacity to be alone without feeling lonely or depressed is nourished by inner resources that build upon the good me-you image of the stage of symbiosis and culminate in what psychoanalysts refer to as "object constancy" at around the age of three.[1] Object constancy refers to the enduring nature of the psychological connection with mother—and later, with important people in general—when they are gone, or when they are not actively meeting one's needs. An emotional connection with a mother who is long dead, with children who are a continent away, with loyal and dear friends we see regularly or only sporadically as busy lives allow, are all manifestations of object constancy. The inner world of ever-present intimacies which continue to nourish and sustain us when we are alone frees us to choose to be alone or to live alone, and to pursue activities which may enrich us even further. A paucity of interests and gratification outside of intense human relationships is often characteristic of dependent men and women.

One of the more important early experiences which leads to the capacity to be alone is that of being alone while being *with* mother, the paradox of being alone together. This is the kind of relating

1. Anna Freud suggests that since the child attains object constancy at about the age of three, this is the best time to start him in nursery school; ". . . separation from mother is less upsetting, he is ready to reach out to new people and to accept new ventures and adventures." That is, because the inner relationship with the mother is secure in the child's mind, he can be away from her without experiencing undue distress. (But see the appendix chapter and the section for working mothers in this book.) "The Concept of Developmental Lines," in P. Neubauer, ed., *The Process of Child Development* (New York: Aronson, 1976), pp. 25–45.

which you may have experienced when you and someone you care for have spent an evening reading, each engrossed in your own book but very much sensing the presence of the other. The child who is beginning to emerge as a separate person has this same sort of experience as he plays on the floor with his toys while mother reads or knits, or works about the house. Even though there may be no interaction, there is a sense of being together, a sense of relatedness.

The need for the actual physical presence of the mothering person in order to maintain this experience of relatedness gradually diminishes with the growth of understanding and memory. The child becomes capable of protecting himself from the distress of separation from the mother by actively recalling her to mind, by using his store of memories and good feeling to maintain the emotional connection with her. As one analyst[2] put it, "The child . . . begins to 'live' a bit less in exclusive response to the outer world; he lives a bit more in his mind."

The capacity to be alone also comes about through the process of learning to do for the self what mother once had to do. An example of this is the kind of caretaking that provides emotional security in the face of stress. When mother isn't available, the young child begins to find ways to do these things for himself. He reaches for his teddy bear or his blanket and comforts and soothes himself with it. This is a very important step. He now actively does for himself what he previously passively experienced his mother doing for him.[3] After a time, the young child outgrows his need for the teddy bear or the blanket and develops within himself, at a symbolic level, resources for the kind of comforting that he derived from the external supports. It is like having a loving mother within one's self. The self-sufficiency that develops draws its substance from the capacity to love and to treasure what one has been given, however, and not from a denial of the importance of others.

The individual who has not developed these inner psychological resources, the inner good mother, may turn to outside sources of comfort such as food, drugs, alcohol, or casual sexual encounters, all

2. Joseph D. Lichtenberg, "The Development of the Sense of Self," *Journal of the American Psychoanalytic Association* 23, no. 2 (1975): pp. 453–84.

3. Marian Tolpin, "On the Beginnings of a Cohesive Self," *The Psychoanalytic Study of the Child,* vol. 26 (New York: Quadrangle Books, 1971).

of which he will use much as the small child uses his teddy bear when mother isn't available. Developing these inner resources is a problem that such an individual will have to deal with if he looks to psychotherapy for help with his problems in living.

When the treatment goes well, the therapist functions for a time as a substitute good mother. At first patients report such experiences as, "I think about you and what you would say to me if you were there." "I carry you around in my pocket and take you out when I need you." Gradually this inner experience of the good therapist-mother becomes an integral part of the self, and the same patient will report, "I no longer consciously think about you at such times, but seem able to make myself feel better. It seems to happen almost automatically."

BEING ME AND LOVING YOU

Adults who are fortunate enough to have come to this point, whether early in life by virtue of a healthy constitution coupled with good parenting, or later on through direct confrontation of the problems inherent in being and loving, experience an enviable freedom and pleasure in their relationships.

Connie and Paul are two such people. They both have strongly defined tastes, opinions, styles, and interests of their own. Their friends often assume that there must be power conflicts between them and that privately one must surely dominate the other. Yet their life together is characterized by an easy and spontaneous flow, a give-and-take, that allows for the authenticity and autonomy of each, as well as for the pleasures of sharing.

Their home reflects their relationship. Each has space that is his or her own and which reflects the individuality of their tastes. Other rooms are a hodgepodge of things they both like which fit together. For these rooms they have one rule—neither buys anything the other can't at least live with comfortably. Self-expression is voluntarily limited when it would constitute an assault on the other. Because each has a strong sense of his or her fundamental autonomy, Connie and Paul are comfortable with their separateness. They do not have to cling to each other in complusive togetherness in order to experience their ongoing emotional connection. Neither feels deserted or resentful at the other's wish to have his or her own time and space.

However, the commitment that each has made to their life together has top priority. Luckily it is a commitment that allows each the freedom to be as well as to love. For example, each can take pleasure in the other's enthusiasms without feeling that he or she has to be enthusiastic about the same thing, or that his or her own enthusiasms must be relinquished. Furthermore, since neither has to defend against domination of the other or pretend infallibility in order to maintain self-esteem, they can turn to each other with trust when either needs comforting. In Connie's and Paul's giving and taking there is a mutuality that is possible simply because it is love, and not power, that connects them.

Unlike the husband of the total woman, Paul does not need Connie's adulation or submission to feel good as a person and as a man. And unlike the total woman, Connie does not have to connive and masquerade to get what she wants and needs. They do not have to manipulate and countermanipulate to get power and dependency needs met. Their relationship is just the opposite of those based upon dependency needs and built around role playing according to a predetermined script. Neither is burdened with the responsibility of maintaining the other's self-esteem or sense of self. And unlike those who have to maintain the myth of perfection in their relationship, Connie and Paul can fight and resolve the archaic issues of being and loving when these issues become reactivated, as they do for everyone from time to time.

The fact that perfection is a myth that can only be maintained at great cost to the individual as well as to a relationship confronts us with the realities of imperfection.

In the best of relationships there is always some conflict or tension from time to time, which has to be resolved. What is at issue is the nature of the resolution. Does it enhance or interfere with being and/or loving? Coming to terms with the fact that there may be no perfect solution is an essential aspect of constructing a life that allows for both.

CHAPTER 9

BEING AND LOVING IN AN IMPERFECT WORLD

YOU MAY HAVE BEEN experiencing a sense of personal failure as you have been reading this book, recognizing that you have not been able to achieve an ideal integration of being and loving in your life. You may have taken this as an indication that there is something wrong with you, or with your husband, wife, or lover. You may be finding it just as hard to accept the imperfectibility of relationships as it is to accept your own personal imperfection.

The renunciation of the ideal of a perfect self is a prerequisite for authentic being, while a renunciation of the ideal of a perfect other is a prerequisite for authentic loving. In a parallel way, the reality of the imperfectibility of relationships in terms of being and loving, and the need for repeated conflict resolution, must also be accepted as inevitable and unavoidable. For only with this kind of acceptance can we manage not to overreact to this conflict with bitterness or discouragement, or with anger and blame.

It is not easy to give up our hopes and ideals for a perfectible world—to confront the realities that we do not live happily forever after, that we will not be rewarded or compensated for our suffering, that conflict is inevitable, and that some problems have no good solutions—only less bad ones.[1]

The concept of an ideal resolution of the conflict between being and loving would imply that there is such a perfectible balance in which they can fully coexist at all times. However, like most ideals, this kind of balance is rarely, if ever, achieved. Even in the happiest of relationships, the conflict rears its head again and again, to be resolved once more. Someone's privacy is not adequately respected. Someone is pressured to go to a movie he or she doesn't want to see. Someone feels misunderstood or inadequately responded to. There is a clash of moods. One wants to make love and the other is preoccupied with problems.

What are your own personal experiences with this kind of conflict? How do you handle those situations? Perhaps you can put disappointment and blame aside long enough to consider ways in which you might be able realistically to bring both experiences into your life.

Whatever your own unique solution, it will have to be in harmony with the person you are—your temperament and rhythms, your interests and tastes, the demands and responsibilities which you must meet. And it will have to take into consideration the same factors in the lives of people who are important to you. Your solution will have to be tailor-made to your own personal way of life.

Lillian Evans is retired and lives alone. She is well aware of her struggle between being and loving. She has struggled for most of her life to bring them into some kind of workable balance. She knew that the experience of intimacy and deep friendship was terribly important for her. Yet she also realized that she could only fully experience her own identity when she was alone.

Lillian has a strong sense of herself but is basically shy and

1. Dr. Roy Schafer describes four basic attitudes toward reality: the comic vision, the romantic vision, the tragic vision, and the ironic vision. He emphasizes the importance of the ironic vision which allows one to confront reality and the imperfections of the world without romanticizing or dramatizing them. It implies a greater detachment and a sense of "that's the way it is." Everything cannot always work out well. But sometimes it can. A clear view of reality enables us to know the difference. *A New Language for Psychoanalysis* (New Haven, Conn.: Yale University Press, 1976).

reluctant to put herself forward. She also tends to lend herself as an empathetic ear for others—her role in her relationship with her father, and one that led her into one of the "helping professions." Thus, in many relationships, she finds herself fading into the background. But she is no loner. She likes being with people and cares deeply about those within the inner circle of her life. She expresses a need for an even balance of being alone and being with others.

She has been able to bring off this resolution because of her ability to be alone without being anxious or depressed. A combination of an "inner good mother," with pleasure in the use of her own intellect and talents, makes for contentment and fulfillment when she is by herself. Her solution to her conflict is in harmony with her "shy and noncombative" nature. It entails alternately moving toward people and moving away from them. Although she could not bring about an ideal resolution of her dilemma, she did work out one that brought both dimensions—being and loving—into her life. Her capacity to be alone made her unique answer possible.

In some ways, Don is like Lillian. He needs to be alone from time to time to feel fully connected with his own being. However, he would really hate to live alone. It would feel too much like his days at boarding school where he was sent when his mother died. He was seven years old, small, and rather timid. He didn't make friends easily because of his shyness, and he experienced terrible homesickness.

He determined to marry young and to raise a large family. That way he would always be surrounded by people whom he loved and who loved him. Despite the dependent quality of this arrangement, he loved his wife and fully appreciated the person she was, and he enjoyed the general family give and take in which he genuinely and spontaneously participated.

But at times Don would feel overwhelmed by the hubbub of his home, and would begin to feel increasingly cut off from himself and his own thoughts. Then he would find himself predominately reacting to the external environment rather than to any sense of what came from within. At these times he would feel an intense need to be alone in order to regain his feelings of being centered within himself.

So Don constructed his private sanctuary. He built a room that was only for him—designed it, furnished it, and decorated it. No one else was allowed in except by invitation. He might leave it to have a cup of coffee with his wife, and then go back to immerse himself in his stamp collection, happy as a clam and feeling warm and content in the close proximity to those he loved.

Don used space and seclusion as a way of maintaining his sense of connection with his own being. The loving attachment was always present, and he could move out toward expression of it when he needed or wanted to. His solution was possible because his wife Lucy was extremely self-reliant and never at a loss for interests of her own. She didn't feel rejected or abandoned because of Don's need to be alone; at those times she drew upon her own resources.

We might accurately predict that Don would face a crisis if he were to lose his family, particularly his wife. But his strong pull toward people and his pleasure in participating in group activities would probably motivate him to fill up his world once again. Even now he talks about opening up his home to foreign students when his children grow up and move away.

For other couples, the resolution of the conflict between being and loving doesn't go so smoothly. And yet, with an atmosphere of basic goodwill, they can negotiate a solution that is at least o.k., if not ideal.

Tim worked under considerable pressure in his law office. He felt a need to unwind at the end of the day. For him this meant regaling his wife Pamela at great length with the details of his day. She often felt this as a demand that she become an ear on legs, and sometimes felt as though she herself were invisible. She was just as tired as Tim and would have liked to be on the receiving end rather than giving. End-of-day crises were frequent—angry explosions and accusations of nonlove and noncare. It became clear that something had to be done when their conflict began to escalate and spread to other aspects of their lives. There were more and more fights about who should yield to whom.

Finally they decided that they had better negotiate if their relationship were to survive. They began with an agreement that each was to be allotted ten minutes of wind-down and complaint time when they got home from work, and then the subject would be dropped. They would then fix dinner together.

Despite the apparently oversimplistic nature of their solution, it comprised a definitive statement that the being of each was important to the relationship and that unless they attended to that principle, loving didn't have much of a chance. Negotiating and taking turns became a useful device for maintaining an optimum balance between being and loving for Tim and Paula.

There are many different ways to live a life. The full life is one in which there is a place for both being me and loving you. Sometimes the people involved can achieve an optimum balance for themselves as did Don and Lucy, and Tim and Paula. Sometimes an individual finds his or her own balance in a single life, as Lillian did.

But sometimes there is an imbalance which the individual or individuals seem unable to remedy by themselves. The imbalance may be the consequence of significant problems left over from the first three years of life. Chronic anger in response to feeling one's selfhood or identity being wiped out, or loneliness because of an absence of loving connections, may interfere with the achieving of a tolerable balance between the two experiences. This is the time to consider looking for help.

Sometimes that help may entail coming to terms with the unhappy reality that there can be no resolution of the conflict within the established relationship. In an imperfect world some problems have no solution. If either Tim or Paula had been unwilling or unable to negotiate and to compromise, their relationship could not have survived except in the form of two people perennially battling to be seen and heard. Sometimes a person feels unable to negotiate because of problems left over from the power pivot. For them, negotiation is tantamount to defeat, and defeat means humiliation. The partner will surely be hated for that.

Giving up unrealistic hope is necessary before real hope can enter our lives. That is, when we come to recognize what is realistically attainable, we can work toward that goal with some real hope of success.

Coming to terms with personal imperfection is a prerequisite for a good enough resolution of the conflict between being and loving.

The protagonists of the great tragedies were doomed by their one "tragic flaw." Othello was a man who had everything—power, wealth, honor, and the love of a beautiful woman. Iago exploited Othello's tragic flaw, his jealousy, and so brought about his downfall. For Caesar it was ambition, "a grievous fault, and grievously hath Caesar answered it." Sometimes we view the failure of the other to understand us and love us perfectly as his or her tragic flaw.

I have sat with individuals who agonized over the task of accepting the imperfection of their parents. To do so would mean giving up hope for that perfect love and understanding. Yet it could not be until they could take that step that they could experience their own love for that parent. The anger of frustration constitutes too great a barrier to the good feelings.

Some years ago, finally giving up the ghost of that struggle myself, I turned to my mother and said, "I don't think you ever will really understand me." She answered with tears in her eyes, "I don't think I ever will." With the mutual acknowledgment and acceptance of the realistic limits of what we could share, I was able to put down my cudgel and to take a good look at this little old lady across from me. I could forgive her for her imperfections, and I could see and appreciate her for who she was and for what she had really given me.

What have been your hopes and expectations in reading this book? Have you anticipated that it would provide the solution to your conflict between being and loving, that it would provide a ready-made answer to the question, "How can I be in a close relationship with another human being without losing myself? How can I have intimacy and still preserve my identity?"

And how have you reacted to the reality that there is no such simple answer?

Are you able to accept the fact that you will most likely have to continue to struggle with the inevitable conflict between being and loving, and that your resolution, whatever it may be, will entail some cost, some renunciation, and will stir up anxiety, guilt, remorse, or grief from time to time? And with the articulation of the dilemma, its realities, and the built-in impossibility of an *ideal* resolution, are you able to begin to struggle toward one that will work for you?

CHAPTER 10

HOW IS IT WITH YOU?

THE PAST chapters have described the early developmental factors which contribute to the conflict between being and loving (or between autonomy and dependency). The conflict is intrinsic to the process of growth and cannot be prevented, even by the best of parenting. We all come to our adult lives with some of its derivatives.

This chapter turns to you. It asks questions which may enable you to assess where you are with issues of being and loving and to define the nature of your problem if you have one. It will offer suggestions which may enhance your ability to take steps toward a better resolution of your conflict as well. Whether this process is one we undertake by ourselves or with the assistance of a psychotherapist, the issues will be the same.

WHAT YOU CAN DO FOR YOURSELF:
TAKING INVENTORY

One of the things you can do for yourself is to take inventory in order to clarify where you stand with respect to being and loving. Where are your vulnerabilities? How do you protect yourself? What price do you pay for this protection?

What about attachments? Have you resolved your conflict between being and loving by denying the wish for intimacy? Do you
want to integrate this experience in your life? Which of the following
comes closest to your experience of emotional attachments?

1. I have no attachments and do not know what it is to have one.
2. I form attachments to animals but not to people. Animals are
   safer. They make no demands on me to be other than who I
   am.
3. I form attachments to people on the basis of what I want them
   to be. For a while they become the ideal parents or family I
   never had but always wanted. But inevitably they disappoint
   me; they fail to live up to my ideal. That's when I transfer
   them from my list of people who are all good to my list of
   those who are all bad. For some reason I have a very short list
   of people who are all good and a very long list of those who
   have let me down.
4. I form attachments but break them off at the first sign of anger
   in me or in the other person. I cannot be angry and still
   maintain the feeling of connection with someone else.
5. I make attachments but break them off when I experience
   pressure not to be me. Even though this may not actually be
   the case, this is what I experienced with my parents and I
   expect the same from others. I may well see these demands
   when they are not actually there. I would rather terminate the
   relationship than assert myself within it. I am afraid of the
   consequences of such self-assertion.
6. I make attachments, but they are based on my dependency
   needs, and sooner or later I come to resent the other person
   because she or he has become too important to me and then I
   end up feeling as though I am in their power. They may not
   actually be trying to exert control over me, but it feels as
   though they are because what they say or do determines how I
   feel about me.
7. I make attachments through my false self. As a result they
   seen unreal. No matter how well things seem to go between
   me and someone else I have a secret fear that the other person

will abandon me if he or she finds out what I am really like, or if I express what is really going on inside me. No matter how well the relationship goes, I feel as though I have nothing because the real me is not participating in the interaction.

8. I make attachments, but before long the only thing that seems to matter is who has power over whom. When this happens, I find little pleasure or love in the relationship.

9. _____

(Maybe you can add your own version here.)

You may want to try to take more risks in moving toward people. Perhaps awareness of the source and nature of the distress or displeasure you feel in intimate relationships will enable you to cope with these feelings.

The struggle to maintain an attachment goes hand in hand with the struggle to remain connected with your real self. Here are some guidelines for assessing problems which you may have in remaining so connected.

1. I don't really have a sense of myself. I don't have that gut level conviction that I am, that I exist. I don't know what I want or what I feel most of the time. I'm used to letting others tell me what and who I am, and what I should or shouldn't do. Sometimes I become confused because I receive so many contradictory directives. I gave up therapy because I couldn't tell whether the things my therapist said about me were actually so or not, and I only felt more confused.

2. I do have a sense of me, but feel I have to keep an emotional distance between myself and others in order to preserve it. Attachments are a threat to my sense of identity and to my autonomy. I avoid them.

3. My real self is a secret self—sometimes even from me. I have constructed an image which I present to the world, to people close to me as well as those who are more distant. Others look at me and think I have it made. But I know it's all an illusion and sometimes I feel alone and frightened.

4. I cover my real self and present the kind of image I know will get attention of some kind, perhaps sympathy if not love. I

hate having to play the "sickie" (or helpless) even though it does get me what I want. I have no respect for myself, and I resent the others who respond to me as the cripple I tell them I am—even though I set it up this way.

5. I push my real self aside. I am afraid of making others angry with me by not being what I think they want me to be, because I am so dependent upon them. I feel as though I am in their control and resent them because of this.

6. I only feel like my real self when I am angry and stand in opposition to someone else. I need to fight in order to feel separate. Sometimes this means I have to say "no" to something I really want. Sometimes this means I have to defeat people who are trying to help me.

7. _____

(Maybe you can add your own version here, also.)

HOW TO FIND YOUR SELF

A rather natural question to ask at this point would be, "How do I go about getting in touch with the real me? If I knew how, I would."

Sometimes confronting the real self may evoke considerable guilt, shame, or anxiety. It may mean looking at aspects of one's self that one may wish to disown. It may mean experiencing feelings which we fear may overwhelm us. These potential dangers stand as a barrier to the process of self-discovery. Coming to grips with the nature of these dangers—real or fantasied—sometimes has to come first, before the individual can feel safe enough to pursue the discovery process. This is often an important aspect of psychotherapy. But if you want to go ahead on your own, here are a few techniques you may find helpful.

I AM A PERSON WHO ——

If you were asked to describe yourself, what would you say? Where would you begin? A useful technique is to draw a list of statements, all starting with the phrase, "I am a person who ———."

When someone cannot even get started with this task, I might suggest beginning with such simple statements as, "I am a person who likes chocolate ice cream." Gradually the self-defining goes into deeper and possibly more painful areas. The capacity to be honest and to relinquish, at least momentarily, the image of the idealized self will determine the effectiveness of this exercise. Being in touch with yourself and having full access to your own inner resources requires awareness of and owning of all aspects of yourself, including those you don't like very much. Only with this process can one achieve a sense of unification and integration. It is a process which takes place more slowly and over a longer period of time in psychotherapy. Sitting down and making a complete list is not always so easy.

OWNING THE DISOWNED

Splitting other people into either all good or all bad makes it impossible to maintain an attachment with them, since all real relationships inevitably have both positive and negative moments. As long as the other person is a constructed ideal or essentially a fantasy, whatever connection we have with him or her will be neither a valid nor an enduring one.

In the same way, the need to split off and repress or deny aspects of ourself which would threaten our self-esteem makes it impossible to have a firm connection with the real self. Denying or repressing feelings and attitudes that we are afraid will get out of control or are afraid will alienate others or will damage our self-esteem in some way is one way to handle the reality that we are *all* a mixture of good and bad, however we may define these qualities. The qualtity "bad" implies something different for different people. For some individuals, "bad" is

1. Being angry
2. Being a show-off
3. Having imperfect judgment
4. Being sexual
5. Having wishes of one's own

6. Showing or feeling tenderness (equated with weakness)
7. Being emotional (also equated with weakness)
8. Being ambitious
9. _____ (add your own)

Women are more likely to disown their ambition and assertiveness because these qualities have for so long been characterized as "unfeminine." On the other hand, I have met some young women recently who are ashamed of their wish to marry and have a family because ambition and assertiveness have become "shoulds" in the women's movement.

Men, on the other hand, are more likely to disown their tenderness and emotionality because these qualities have been characterized as "unmanly."

Social values and stereotypes are one source of disintegrating pressure. Parents may unwittingly interfere with the process of integration of all aspects of self in the early years. A parent may say to the child who is misbehaving in some way, "You're not being yourself today!" The goal of the mother or father may be to maneuver the child into behaving more acceptably. The message that approved-of behavior is that of the real self while disapproved-of behavior is not that of the real self contributes to the splitting off of different aspects of the child's personality.

A similar kind of disintegrating pressure is reported by men and women who begin to grow and change as the result either of therapy or of their own spontaneous maturation. Old friends and family may react to their changed behavior with, "What's the matter with you? You're not being yourself today." This is especially likely to be the reaction to new angry or assertive behavior. This failure to validate the individual's experience of himself is very controlling, and is often enough to coerce a return to old and familiar patterns of interaction. It is not always easy to rediscover and own and integrate the many facets of one's own personality.

Are you surprised at some of the statements you have made about the person you are? Have you found this exercise to be more difficult than you had anticipated? How did you react to statements you did not like or approve of?

DISCOVERING YOUR EXPERIENCING SELF

The experiencing self is not the same as *what* one experiences, but the sense of the self who is having the experience. The capacity to focus upon the experiencing self is vital to the process of trying to discover and connect with the self.[1]

When somebody tells me, "I only feel confused," I may ask him to focus on the self who is having the experience of being confused, rather than on the confusion itself. People often become so focused upon the experience that they lose touch with the experiencer, that is, the self.

In the case of anxiety, one may become so overwhelmed by the feelings that he loses sight of the self who is feeling. This adds to the distress. Then, in an attempt to push away the unpleasant experience—to get rid of the anxiety in this instance—the individual further loses touch with the self.

An experience will not be so frightening, nor will one feel so helpless in the face of it, if one does not lose touch with the self who is doing the experiencing. It is important to be able to say, "Whether I am afraid, or sad, or confused, I still have a firm sense of my own continuity, my own continuing existence, at the center of these difficult moments."

We can also get in closer touch with our real self through the body, through our conscious thoughts, and through our dreams.

YOUR BODILY SELF

The infant's first awareness of self is the awareness of its physical self—of the body and the sensations from within it as well as from the skin and the sense organs.

If you sometimes feel your sense of self slipping away under certain kinds of stress, you can reconnect with it through the

1. Rollo May writes: "The self is not merely the sum of the various 'roles' one plays—it is the capacity by which one *knows* he plays these roles; it is the center from which one sees and is aware of these so-called different 'sides' of himself." *Man's Search for Himself* (New York: Dell, 1973), p. 91.

medium of your bodily self. You can try to become aware of your breathing, of the feeling of your feet on the floor, or of your rear end where it is in contact with the chair. By focusing your awareness on your bodily self, you can reestablish the location of your identity within the boundaries of your own skin.

I have suggested that people start this exercise by focusing on their own belly button, the first indicator of separateness from mother and thus the first definition of one as an individual. One young woman who was struggling against the loss of contact with her self in the context of pressure from other people, misheard me to say that she should focus on the umbilical cord. This misunderstanding was a manifestation of her inability at that moment either to perceive or to accept her own separateness.

A second step of the belly-button exercise is to focus on parts of the body at increasing distances from the navel and, with each one, to experience the connection between that part of the body and the belly button. For instance I might say, "Now feel your knee. Feel just above it. Feel higher. Feel all the way to your belly button. Now back to your knee. Now experience the connection between them." Ultimately the aim of the exercise is to feel real at a bodily level, facilitating the integration of all parts of the self into a cohesive and unitary whole.

LISTENING TO YOURSELF

One can get more closely in touch with one's self by listening to what is going on in one's head as well as in one's body. Listening to one's voice and one's conscious thoughts is one way to do this. Listening to the messages from our dreams is another.

Turning an ear—literally—to our own voice and our own words can be done by speaking into a tape recorder and then listening to what we have recorded. We can also do this by writing a letter to ourself and then reading it with the same care and attention we would give to a letter from someone else.

Talking to one's self has often been equated with being a little bit crazy, but it can be a very valuable technique for discovering what is going on in our own head. Our tone of voice, the emotional concomitant to the words as we speak them, and the emergence of thoughts and ideas we may have been unaware of, reveal to us aspects of ourself which may be giving us difficulty. Sometimes it is difficult to grasp and articulate the thoughts and fantasies which float around in our head. Putting them into words can be quite revealing. And by putting them into words we gain a significant measure of control and mastery of our own psychological processes. Gestalt therapists make extensive use of such techniques, "giving a voice" to one's tears, to one's sudden headache, to one's clenched teeth. Listening to the messages from within the self, which are expressed in a wide variety of ways by translating them into words, puts one in closer touch with one's self and facilitates the integration of conflicting aspects of the self.

Paying attention to our dreams is another way to listen to our own voice.[2] In dreams we speak in symbols and metaphors, so that the language of our dreams may need some translation before we can understand what we are, in effect, trying to say to ourselves. It is because our dreams are such a valuable clue to what is going on in our own insides that many therapists make translating them such an important part of therapy.

Dreams can be approached in a number of ways. Basic to them all is the recognition that abstract ideas must be expressed in visual symbols, and the assumption that the dream is a kind of metaphor, a symbolic expression of a wish, a fear, a conflict—some aspect of one's own self and one's own life. Even though other people are actors in our dreams, we are the ones who tell them what to say and what to do. We write the script. Their words come from our own heads.

---

2. Everyone dreams, but not everyone remembers his or her dreams, or even the fact that they dream. Dr. David Foulkes reports research findings about dream recallers as compared to nonrecallers. Those who remembered their dreams were found to be less conformist, less self-controlled, and less defensive. The forgetting of dreams or denial of dreaming, then, is related to the *extensive* use of repression as a defense. *The Psychology of Sleep* (New York: Scribner's, 1966).

Sometimes the dream can be understood as representing *some denied and repressed aspect of the self* which is nonetheless the basis for troublesome feelings even though we have no conscious awareness of it. One very competent and independent woman often dreamed about lost kittens. The kittens in her dreams represented the frightened child part of her that had been pushed away very early in life in response to the demands of her parents that she be "a big girl." Seemingly irrational bouts of depression or anxiety could not be understood until they could be connected with the lost-child part of herself.

Sometimes a dream can be understood as a *statement about one's life.* Another woman would frequently dream about houses—houses with many, many rooms, all of them filled with lovely surprises and treasures, but with no people in them. She yearned to share her own inner treasures with someone, but was coming to realize it could not be with the cold and aloof man to whom she was married.

Sometimes dreams represent *wishes.* One man dreamed of flying high above a distant city. His dream told his wish which was not yet fully conscious, to be free of the unhappy life he was in and to make a new one for himself.

And sometimes dreams depict our *dreads and anxieties,* such as the frequent dreams one woman had of tornadoes and tidal waves and hurricanes and earthquakes. In these dreams she would be rushing about frantically trying to protect her children from falling walls or trees. These dreams expressed her intense anxiety over the threatening collapse of her world (her marriage), and the extent to which she feared its destructive potential for her children. And at still another level, it once again expressed the anxiety she had felt as a child over the imminent collapse of her parents' marriage. Her nightmares predated her conscious awareness of these feelings in the present by several years, and until they could be admitted into that awareness, she experienced only nameless anxiety.

Another young woman, at the adult edge of adolescence, often dreamed about bridges, and in these dreams she would be terrified of crossing them. In one dream she sat at a dining table with her family at one end of the bridge. She was struggling with the developmental task of her age—the breaking of the dependent tie with her family. When she came to understand the nature of her anxiety, she was once again able to resume her schooling and the move toward independence which it represented.

To understand your own dreams, think of them as metaphors, as symbols of some aspect or aspects of you, and some aspect or aspects of your life now and in the past. You may appear in one dream in several disguises, each representing one aspect which may be in conflict with one of the others. For instance, you may appear as both adult and child in one dream. You may be present in the dream as a neutral observer standing to one side as well.

Sometimes people we hardly know or people from our distant past come into our dreams and we wonder what on earth they are doing there. You can discover how you have used someone as a symbol by letting yourself focus on what this person brings to mind. For instance, one man dreamed about a girl who was in his class in grammar school. His association was that she was the littlest kid in the class. From there he went on to think about his own littlest kid, his youngest child, and then about himself as the youngest child in the family in which he grew up. As he explored the dream further, he could understand that it was saying something about the feelings he had had (and obviously still did have, unconsciously) about being the youngest and the smallest. He came to understand some reactions he was having at work in his present life, particularly his frustration and anger at not having his ideas listened to just as he had not been listened to and taken seriously in family discussions at the dinner table.

Dreams often take up elements of something that has happened in reality the day before the dream, and use those events as props, weaving into them the issues of one's life as it is experienced in the present and often as this relates to how it was experienced growing up. Present-day situations and relationships stir up feelings from old situations and relationships, particularly when these feelings are still heavily loaded with guilt, anxiety, anger, or conflict.

Your dreams are a key to your inner psychological world, and paying attention to them and coming to understand them will bring you into closer touch with yourself.

PUTTING IT ALL TOGETHER

The life of any given individual has its own internal organization and consistency. What may appear irrational comes to make sense when it is viewed within the context of one's entire life, particularly one's earliest years.

In this chapter your attention has been directed toward different aspects of yourself, including your attitudes and behaviors with respect to emotional attachments, as well as the depth and quality of your connection with the real human being you are.

Putting these bits and pieces together in the context of your own history may promote a further integration, which may, in turn, enable you to come closer to a resolution of your conflict between being and loving.

This task can be approached through the device of writing your autobiography in as great detail as you are able. Check with family for information which you either do not know or which you have long forgotten. As you begin to reconstruct the story of how you got to be the person you are today, try to tie the present to the past, to discover the connecting links.

Although this exercise may promote insight, insight per se is not the primary goal. The writing itself should serve an organizing and integrating function, promoting your sense of personal wholeness and integrity.

You may come to see how issues of being a separate and autonomous person have always been foremost, in conflict with your needs and wish to be close and loving with others. You may become aware how feelings from the power pivot of the second year of your life never really did quiet down, and that you have struggled with feelings of inadequacy and shame ever since then, and have defended yourself against them by retreating to illusions of your own perfection. How did it affect your relationships within your family, with the kids at school, when you started to date, when you got your first job? And now?

The more clearly you delineate yourself as a real live, multi-dimensional human being, the better you will be able to perceive others in the same way. And this is, after all, the most important step in the development of the capacity for authentic being and authentic loving.

WHEN TO SEEK HELP

Check your own experiencing self at this moment. Do you have a sense of having a handle on the issues that may trouble you? Do you have a sense of knowing what to do now that you have defined the problem? Or do you feel overwhelmed and discouraged? Do you experience the need for help in clarifying your problems? For a reliable support in the face of debilitating anxiety or depression? Do you feel yourself only getting in deeper and deeper, unable to resolve your dilemma? If this is the case, then you might consider the alternative of psychotherapy, of seeking the assistance of someone with some expertise in dealing with problems of being and loving.

Whether the major problem is one of making and maintaining psychological attachments, or of experiencing and maintaining one's sense of self, the integration of both of these facets of human experience is the way to the best of all possible worlds, to "being me" and "loving you."

CHAPTER 11

CAN THERAPY HELP?

By NOW YOU HAVE READ about the genesis of being and loving in the life of the individual and how one's adult experience continues to be affected by the inevitable conflict between them.

You may have concluded that your own feelings of anxiety, depression, or chronic anger are related to this conflict. And you may have decided that you would like to talk to someone about it. However, you may also, quite understandably, have some reservations about taking this step.

WHY WITH A THERAPIST?

Psychotherapy provides a unique setting and ambience. It provides a context specifically geared toward change and growth. It provides the support of a to-be-counted-on relationship with someone who is interested in you. And it provides objective confrontation.

The process of change and growth is difficult, and for the most part it comes about not only as the result of introspection and self-understanding. It also comes about as the result of struggling with what we experience in our interactions with others. Just as the child develops the capacities to be and to love *within the context of a relationship,* specifically that with the mothering person of the earliest years, so one needs others with whom to interact in a special way in order to promote growth and development later in life. This is the experiential component of the growth process, whether in therapy or not, and a relationship-as-context-for-growth is one of the major contributions of the therapeutic situation.

It is usually harder to make changes within old and established relationships. They tend to pull us back into old patterns unless the other people involved understand what is happening and are able to participate in the process and to make the kind of complementary shifts that change entails. This is why a marriage may be disrupted when only one member grows and changes. If both partners do not work together, the force of the pull and tug may increase until the relationship becomes unworkable. The growing member tries to pull the partner into a new way of defining the relationship, into new ways of interacting. The nongrowing member drags his or her heels and tries to pull the partner back to the way things used to be. Conjoint marital therapy tries to help both partners grow together.

The same principle applies with respect to an individual vis-à-vis parents. Some parents are able to make the shifts that are necessary to accommodate the growth of a son or daughter. Others exert psychological pressure to keep things as they were. For instance, they withdraw love and become hostile when the young person begins to make noises about moving out of the parental home. The threat of emotional abandonment may, in some cases, be enough to keep the son or daughter in line, and they pay the price of stopped development. In such situations, the growth of the young person may rupture the relationship irreparably, and he or she has to make the painful choice between being and loving. The support of a therapist can make this pain bearable.

By and large, the do-it-yourself approach is difficult in that it lacks the support and reliability of a to-be-counted-on relationship to sustain one through the more difficult times. People in the world at large have needs, motives, plans, and ways of being of their own, and they cannot always be counted on realistically to lend themselves to the service of the extended self-examination and self-discovery that goes with the process of change. They cannot always be expected to bear the burden of the ups and downs of one's feelings, of the preoccupation with one's self and psyche, or of the need for patience and forbearance as one tries and retries new attitudes and behaviors. The therapist endeavors to lend himself or herself to this process as fully as possible, for that is the defined goal of the relationship.

In addition, the human psyche is devilishly clever at the art of self-deception, and the need for a reliable, consistent, honest, nonhostile, and reasonably objective confrontation is an essential component of the change process. This is the function of a therapist, as he or she facilitates the emergence and definition of the self within the context of a trusting and nonexploitative relationship. The patient is helped to become aware of feelings and wishes and to develop an understanding of them as well as to face conflict and find a solution.

BUT ON THE OTHER HAND—

Whatever their motivation to undertake therapy, many people are also reluctant to do so. The source of the reluctance is often closely related to issues of being and loving, such as self-esteem, power, or the fear of loss through change. Coming to terms with the reluctance is often not only the first, but the most important step in the process.

The very fact of "needing" to see a therapist is experienced by some individuals as a failure to live up to their idealized image of themselves as totally capable of solving their own problems. Thus, it constitutes a humiliation. There is potential for further humiliation as a consequence of being seen in a less-than-perfect light by someone else. Who knows what might be revealed in the course of therapy. And crying, of course, is to be avoided at all costs. Big girls (or boys) don't cry!

Others come to the therapy situation already angry at being in a one-down power position. They come to the therapist, and not vice versa. The therapist is in control of the time. The therapist must be paid. They tell the therapist about themselves, but the therapist does not reciprocate. It is reality that therapy is an inherently unequal situation, in spite of the therapist's regard for the patient as a respected equal. The reluctance to get into such a position is enough to deter many people from getting help for their problems of being and loving.

The fear of loss through change relates to both loss of self and loss of important others. People are often concerned that if they change, they will not be themselves anymore, as though changing would make them into someone else. The change of therapy, in fact, aims at helping the individual become more fully himself. Nevertheless, this would still entail a loss of the familiar self, and this may be anxiety provoking.

Some people mistakenly believe that giving up their dependent ties to family means that one can no longer have anything to do with them. There may well be good and healthy aspects of old relationships that need not be thrown away in a desperate attempt to make one's self emotionally independent of them. For it is the *inner relationship,* how we experience it psychologically, that is the crucial one—whether or not one is tied and bound emotionally in the various ways which have been described in this book, if not in actual time and space.

Sometimes the fear of the loss of important others is well justified. This would be true when a spouse or parents cannot tolerate the growth and change of the individual, and the relationship is actually terminated. This real danger is a powerful deterrent to plunging into the therapy situation.

Therapy can also be perceived as a threat to an idealized image of the family. Like other idealized images, they are maintained at the cost of coming to terms with reality. Behind this fear lies the danger that, if the family is viewed realistically, it might be lost. That is, the individual would not be able to fit within it anymore.

In other situations, telling family secrets constitutes a "betrayal," and the guilt about this possibility is enough to keep the person out of therapy.

Whatever the nature of your reluctance to get involved in the therapy process, be sure to talk it over if you do consult someone. Any therapist should be willing to respect your concerns and to explore them further with you. Perhaps this exploration will help you decide to commit yourself to the process in spite of your anxieties.

Once one has overcome the initial reluctance sufficiently to make that first call, the question arises, "Whom do I call?"

CHOOSING A THERAPIST

Most patients find their way to a therapist via direct referral. Either a former patient, a family physician, another therapist, or someone familiar with a particular therapist's work will say, "I think this is someone who can help you." Since there is some degree of preliminary matching of patient to therapist with a personal referral, these arrangements are more likely to work out than picking a name out of a book. The referral is also a recommendation which is based on past performance.

The therapist's credentials are also a consideration. What is this person's training? Is he or she licensed or certified? If not, does he or she work for an accredited agency or clinic? Some indication that this person is accepted by others in the field as competent affords some degree of assurance.

Beyond this, there are a number of different kinds of therapy— different theoretical orientations, different techniques, different therapist styles and values, each of which has its own specific impact on the person looking for help. The age and sex of the therapist are often important in this regard.

THERAPEUTIC GOALS AND STYLES

For the most part, the goal of psychotherapy, regardless of "school" or techniques which may be employed, is essentially a humanistic one. That is, it aims toward a secure and authentic sense of self and self-worth. One can be a behaviorist whose goal is to unlearn maladaptive and self-defeating behavior patterns, a Freudian analyst with a focus on resolving unconscious conflict, or a Gestalt therapist who strives for the integrity and wholeness of the person, and still pursue humanistic goals. Rollo May wrote of existential psychology, ". . . the term demarcates an *attitude,* an approach to human beings, rather than a special school or group. . . it is not a system of therapy but an attitude toward therapy."[1] He points out that every therapist is existential insofar as he or she is a good therapist and is able to grasp the patient in his or her own reality.

Whatever the therapist's particular style and technique of working, it may have both a positive and a negative impact on one. Someone might say, "I wish you would talk more. I feel you leave it all up to me." What is most important is that the therapist be willing to consider as part of the process, exploring the nature of that impact. A therapist who will not do this, who says "take it or leave it," is not likely to be able to help the patient come to terms with his mixed feelings about other relationships either.

This does not mean that the therapist should change the way of working just to make you feel better. This might even be antitherapeutic, depriving you of the necessity and opportunity of coming to grips with your reactions. It's the talking about them that is at issue. Sometimes a therapist can be too nice, and that will not be useful if you are to grow. The patient who wanted the therapist to talk more might use this as a way to avoid the responsibility for what is brought up.

One of these differences is the extent to which a therapist reveals his or her own feelings and reactions. The analytically oriented therapist attempts to maintain an attitude of neutrality, believing that this facilitates the emergence of the kinds of feelings and attitudes that people carry about with them in their heads, and that it facilitates the emergence and growth of the individual's unique and spontaneous self. This neutrality is not the same as indifference, however, although the two are sometimes confused. The analytic

1. Rollo May, "The Emergence of Existential Psychology," in Rollo May, ed., *Existential Psychology* (New York: Random House, 1965), p. 19.

therapist lends himself or herself to the growth of the individual much as the early mother lends herself to the growth of her child.

Other therapists work quite differently, bringing their own feelings and reactions in as an integral aspect of the working relationships. They believe that it is important to function as a model for openness. Some people can make good use of this style of working. Others, however, react to it by giving over direction of themselves to the therapist much as they did originally with parents. The adapting individual will conform to what seems to please and interest the therapist. Sacrificing being in the interest of loving can be acted out in therapy just as everywhere else. Sometimes apparent growth (such as improving one's appearance, going to school, or working for a job promotion) may be little more than a manifestation of adaptation to the goals toward which the therapist is offering encouragement. The goal itself remains irrelevant and achieving it has little impact on the individual one way or the other; pleasing the therapist (parent) is still at the heart of the process. Sometimes the therapist's honest reaction will be experienced as praise or punishment for the individual who relates in this manner.

In choosing a therapist for yourself, it would be helpful for you to do some preliminary assessment of your own reaction tendencies. Which one of these attitudes do you think would be most helpful for you with respect to promoting growth? It might *not* be the one which would necessarily make you feel better, however. Feeling comfortable or gratified in a therapy session is not always necessarily productive.

INSIGHT OR UNDERSTANDING

Different therapists also disagree on the relative importance of insight or understanding vis-à-vis having an experience. Such disagreements obscure the nature of growth and change. For understanding without experience is sterile. Experience without understanding cannot be fully integrated and made a part of the self. Human beings are creatures who seek to find sense and meaning in their experience so that they can extrapolate from it and extend its influence and impact upon their lives.

Experience without understanding, no matter how gratifying or exciting, can be little more than a series of ad hoc situations with no carry-over power. Many people who are habitués of encounter groups or workshops of one sort or another are essentially "group addicts." They experience an emotional high in these groups, but suffer the inevitable letdown, a kind of withdrawal reaction, when they return to the real world. There is no inner change with which to effect change in one's everyday life, but a craving is established for more such experiences, and they go back for a "fix" when the next workshop comes along. They do not understand the meaning of their experience with respect to their own psyche—and therefore they cannot integrate it into their being in harmony with their sense of self. Therapies or therapists who hold out promise of going away feeling marvelous from their sessions should be looked at with question. If your wish to understand as well as to feel is derogated, as with a label of "mind fucking," consider whether this is really the place for you.

Insight or understanding is equally sterile when it is used to avoid experience, and thus to protect us from the anxiety of experience.

Assess your own reaction tendencies with respect to feeling, doing, and thinking. What sort of balance do you think would be most helpful for you?

GROUP THERAPY?

If you think you are the kind of person who might hide behind words, or who might get caught up in trying to please your therapist, even covertly, group therapy may be the therapy of choice for you. Your behavior will be more open to the scrutiny of your peers, and you're not likely to get away with being "teacher's pet" in a group. Problems which stem from sibling rivalry, for example, may not show up in individual therapy where one is an "only child."

The here-and-how social interaction of a therapy group often exposes the ways in which people inject unresolved conflicts from their families into present-day social situations. Some of these would remain hidden in one-to-one therapy unless the individual saw fit to bring them up.

As with other factors in choosing the kind of therapy and therapist, the question of whether it will hinder or facilitate your growth is a prime consideration. Assigning a person to a therapy group, however, is usually the decision of the therapist. That is, the therapist may recommend individual treatment, perhaps for an interim period, even if you believe group therapy would be best. If this is the case, he or she should explain the basis for the decision. This often highlights problems that need to be resolved in individual treatment first.

MALE OR FEMALE?

Whatever problems one has with respect to being and loving, they will emerge with either a male or a female therapist. The male therapist can be related to as though he were mother, and the female therapist can be related to as though she were father. Some people have a fantasy that a woman will provide warmth and love, whereas a man will be cold and intellectual. These are gross stereotypes which have nothing to do with what happens in psychotherapy. Inevitably they will have to be dealt with as the fantasies they are.

By and large it does not matter what the gender of the therapist is—except:

When an individual has *excessive* fear or anger toward either men or women, it is best to start with a therapist of the opposite sex. That is because these feelings will be brought into the therapy situation and will probably prevent progress in the establishment of trust.

One young woman came into my office for the first time and had an immediate strong negative reaction to me because I wore my hair and dressed in the style of her mother. I hope these feelings can be worked with and overcome, as these kinds of overgeneralizations and distortions of reality (for, after all, I wasn't actually her mother) interfere in the outside world as well. However, in this instance, the initial negative feelings were so strong that it made no sense to try to work together. It would have been impossible to build up a trusting relationship.

The opposite situation is also an indication for a therapist of a specific gender—that is, when the individual relates automatically in too cozy and comfortable a manner with either one or the other. Too many built-in positive feelings can be just as much of a deterrent to progress in therapy as too many built-in negative feelings, for they become too precious, and anything that might interfere with them is screened out and not talked about.

Once you have overcome your original ambivalence, you will make the first call and set up an appointment. People generally tend to be very anxious the first session, wondering what they are "supposed to do." Dealing with the fact that there are no supposed-tos (other than to come at your specified hour, do your best to be honest, and pay your bill) is one of the first tasks of therapy. It is most useful to discuss your fears and reluctances at the very start so they can be worked with and resolved. Often the nature of the reluctance is itself the central problem of the individual's life. This is particularly so when it relates to the conflict between being and loving.

PROBLEMS OF BEING AND LOVING IN THERAPY

Inevitably the conflict between attachment and individuation, between dependence and autonomy, between loving and being, will come to light in the therapy relationship itself. Resolution of the conflict in this special setting, then, becomes the nitty-gritty of the work of therapy.

If you have difficulty in making and maintaining attachments, this will come up as an issue with your therapist, but at least it can be openly talked about and dealt with here. One young woman struggled with the belief that if she let herself be at all involved with me, I would take her over and make her into what I wanted her to be. She avoided attachments in general as a way to protect her boundaries and her sense of self.

If you tend to break off your feelings of connection every time your therapist makes you angry by not responding the way you want, if you "pull the plug," this too can be identified and talked about and you can, with his or her help, work to maintain the feeling of connection right on through the anger.

If you sense yourself pulling out when you hear an interpretation as pressure not to be you, as criticism and withdrawal of caring, this too can be talked about and clarified. You can become aware of the kind of misinterpretations you are prone to making in the communication process. Just because your father didn't want you to have a mind of your own does not imply that everyone else has the same attitude, although you may have a tendency to attribute that meaning to their behavior.

You will discover that you and the other person (in this case, your therapist) can be *different* and still be connected. You don't have to be the kind of person he or she is. He doesn't have to agree with you on everything in order to guarantee that you will still go on existing. You can be angry with each other and neither one of you will die.

Or you may become aware of how power issues generate so much resentment in you that you cannot permit yourself to be the recipient of help rather than the giver. You may find yourself needing to defeat your therapist in order to maintain your self-esteem, recognizing that the same thing happens in outside relationships as well. You can talk about your dilemma and, with your therapist's support, untie the knot that binds you.

If you tend to be compliant with what you believe the other person wants from you or needs from you, this attitude and behavior will also emerge in your relationship with your therapist. As this pattern becomes clarified within the therapy situation, your feelings and beliefs can be explored in a way that gives you the courage to take the risk of being more real.

You may come to realize that you set your therapist up as the fountain of all power and knowledge, and try to get her or him to give you the magic solution. Coming to terms with this fantasy and giving up the search for an all powerful rescuer in your life will go hand in hand.

One of the most important tasks in therapy is often that of

learning to tolerate ambivalence in a relationship rather than making the other either all good or all bad. This entails completing the task of healing the split at the end of the power pivot stage of development. This will be carried over to other relationships in which the other can finally be experienced as a single individual toward whom one feels sometimes angry and sometimes loving.

Throughout therapy, the process of self-discovery will continue to facilitate the integration of the self into a unified whole with a healthy, reality-oriented self-esteem replacing unworkable illusions of perfection.

The list of problems deriving from the developmental stages of the first three years of life could go on and on. Perhaps you have been able to identify some of these in your own life or in the lives of people you know. How they are resolved will determine the quality of our life, be it alone or with another, be it imprisoned in the citadel of the self or secure enough to move toward a loving attachment. The struggle to bring being into harmony with loving, to maintain the sense of our own identity and integrity and, at the same time, to appreciate the wholeness of another person whom we love is a struggle that begins in the nursery and is usually with us throughout our lifetime. Sometimes its resolution begins in the therapist's consultation room. We hope a synthesis of the two will not be beyond anyone's hope or expectation in spite of impediments to it which have been left over from the early years of life.

APPENDIX:
NOT FOR PARENTS ONLY

THIS APPENDIX is for the reader who is a parent or who is planning to be one. It is quite obvious that a child does not develop in a vacuum and that something quite special is required of you if that development is to go well—particularly with respect to being and loving.[1] It is also quite obvious that you are a person, too, and that you will have to deal with the demands of parenthood as they affect your own state of being and loving.

STAGES OF PARENTING

Parenting includes nurturance, protection, teaching, and fostering independence in all mammals.[2] Human parents also inculcate

1. Erik Erikson refers to the quality of "generativity" as a developmental task of adult life. Generativity is primarily the concern for establishing and guiding the next generation. It also refers to creativity in other spheres of activity. Erik Erikson, *Childhood and Society,* 2nd ed. (New York: Norton, 1963).
2. Charles Kaufman, "Biologic Considerations of Parenthood," in E. J. Anthony and T. Benedek, eds., *Parenthood: Its Psychology and Psychopathology* (Boston: Little, Brown, 1970), pp. 3–55.

values and norms and provide training in certain specific kinds of behavior. They serve as models for adult roles which the child uses to form his concept of himself and his place in society. And, it is hoped, they also foster in him appropriate self-regard.[3]

Each stage of your child's development which was described earlier in this book will call upon a specific and corresponding attitude on your part. Your growth and change as a parent will parallel that of your child as a person. Throughout this process your attitudes and behavior will affect him, and his attitudes and behavior will affect you and the quality of your parenting.[4]

Because of the interactive nature of the parent-child relationship, we can see that a child is not a passive lump of clay to be molded by the parent. He is an active participant in his own developmental process. Different kinds of children call forth different kinds of responses.[5] A boisterous, active child is more likely to evoke limit-setting responses. An orderly, self-reliant child is more likely to evoke autonomy-promoting responses. A timid child is more likely to evoke caretaking responses. Yet all three have the same basic requirement for healthy emotional development. That is, each goes through the process of attachment to symbiosis, and through the process of separation and individuation. As a parent, you will want to keep these principles in mind, even as you respond to the temperamental needs of your child.

When your child is going through the attachment process and moving toward becoming one with mother, you (if you are the mother) will be under maximal pressure to put your own wishes, moods, feelings, and needs aside to tend to your baby. This is the time when your goal will be to meet his needs, to foster the attach-

3. Gerald Handel, "Sociological Aspects of Parenthood," ibid., pp. 87–105.

4. René Spitz writes of "mutual cuing," the process of reciprocal influence which characterizes mother-child interaction in the first year of life. The concept of mutual cuing can be applied to later stages of development as well. *The First Year of Life* (New York: International Universities Press, 1965).

5. Dr. Alexander Thomas and Dr. Stella Chess have studied the relationship between an infant's innate temperament and subsequent development. They describe (1) the difficult child, (2) the easy child, and (3) the slow-to-warm-up child, and how to handle each most effectively. *Temperament and Development* (New York: Brunner/Mazel, 1977).

ment process, and to create an atmosphere of trust and minimal tension. If you are the father, your support is needed to help your wife through this period so that she, herself, does not become emotionally depleted. It may be a tough time for you, as you are likely to be mostly on the giving end. If never before, it will be evident now that the honeymoon is over!

Before long your child will begin to move toward defining himself as separate from you in many little ways, such as wanting to hold his own bottle or spoon. Now the balance begins to shift a little. You are still needed as in the earlier months, but now you must begin to encourage and support these moves toward independence. It is no longer appropriate for you to try to match your rhythm so perfectly to that of the child. You begin to make small demands: he has to wait for the bottle. He is no longer on demand feeding as in those earlier weeks and months. Chances are he has moved toward a regular schedule himself, as well. At any rate, he now hears no-no from you more frequently. As your baby comes to realize that he cannot control you by his will, he becomes more and more aware that you and he are separate.

Father now becomes increasingly important. As you have played with your baby and helped with the caretaking, he has also formed a bond with you. You become most important now in the process of becoming two. You are a source of security and trust that enables him to move further away from mother without becoming overwhelmed by separation anxiety.

Throughout the process of becoming two, which includes the power pivot, your child will experience conflict between his dependency needs and his autonomy needs. Dependency needs are related to loving in that both move one toward the other, whereas autonomy needs are related to being, in that both emphasize separateness. Their conflicts are also parallel. You will be called upon to support both the conflicting needs—which can be tricky if not actually impossible at any given moment. Then you have to decide which is more critical. If your child is upset or distraught over some difficulty, clearly he needs comfort and support. If he is trying to build his blocks into a tower, clearly he needs encouragement without interference.

In any event, the balance continues to shift gradually, with you doing less and less for your child as he is able to do more and more for himself. Helpful parents have the emotional flexibility to make these shifts. They are not locked into either one stance or the other because of their own particular psychological needs. They do not need their child to stay dependent nor to become prematurely autonomous.

It will also be up to both fathers and mothers to set the kind of limits that will mitigate the normal narcissism of the very small child. Others are people who count, too. "No, you can't have the doll. The doll belongs to Susie." This step is essential to the capacity to love, for loving entails valuing others as real persons. The self-centered individual who relates to others in terms of how they fit in with his need system cannot really love.

This requires a further shift from you. Now, not only are you not responding to your child's every demand, but you are making demands on him. Many modern parents are appropriately concerned with the individuality of their child. However, in the earliest years it is equally important to provide guidance and control. Inadequate structuring of the child's environment may lead to a less secure inner-self structure. In such circumstances, individuality, paradoxically, cannot be well developed.[6] The psychological well-being of the child requires parents who are secure in their educational role as well as in their loving and supporting role.

As with the balance between dependency and autonomy, there must be a balance between demands for renunciation of narcissism and adequate meeting of the child's needs for self-esteem and self-expression. If he feels valued and validated by you (and thus, eventually able to value and validate himself), he will be able to give up being kingpin of the household. He won't have to hold on to infantile illusions of omnipotence. Growth-facilitating parents are able to keep sight of the needs which the child is in the process of outgrowing at the same time as they are anticipating and moving toward the child's next developmental challenges.

6. Therese Benedek, "The Family as a Psychologic Field," in *Parenthood: Its Psychology and Psychopathology*, pp. 109–35.

Whatever the objective demands of parenthood, those which relate to the expected developmental requirement of the child, parenting has its unique and subjective effects on every mother and father.

PARENTS ARE PEOPLE, TOO

We bring to marriage and parenthood the personality which was built up over our own early years.[7] This includes how we interacted with our own parents and other important people in our world. There is a tendency to identify our child with our parent and to make certain assumptions and to take certain attitudes on the basis of this identification. This is why there is often a similarity between the quality of parent-child relationships from one generation to the next.[8]

The experience of parenthood can actually be a growth-promoting one. Our own early conflicts tend to be reactivated in our relationship with our child. This gives us a chance to confront these conflicts with the mental and psychological equipment of the adult and thus, to resolve them. Many parents with several children will report that they are aware of how much more mature they were in their parenting of the later children. The firstborn often has the dubious honor of being the one with whom the conflict is worked out. Not all parents do grow in this way, however, but continue to play out the conflict in a repetitive manner just as they did as children vis-à-vis their own parents.

Just as you have an impact on the developing self of your child, so he or she has an impact on you. This impact may generate stress if and when it touches upon vulnerable aspects of your own self, especially those which may relate to your conflict between being and loving. For instance, your sense of being may be placed in jeopardy when your boundaries and autonomy are suspended in order to meet the demands of parenting your newborn infant. And you may lose

7. Ibid., p. 110.
8. Introduction, *Parenthood: Its Psychology and Pathology*, p. xxi.

touch with your loving feelings for your child when your anger gets the upper hand. If so, you are like many other parents.

If you are the mother of a new or almost new baby, there may be times when you feel as though your boundaries and your sense of separateness becomes blurred with the extent to which you give yourself to tending to the needs of your infant. Even your sleeping and eating rhythm is set aside in favor of rocking a fretful child or for the 2:00 A.M. feeding.

There may be times when both mother and father react with frustration and anger to the limits placed on your autonomy by the responsibilities of parenthood. No more spur-of-the-moment weekend camping trips. No more easy, "Let's eat out and go to a show." Even if you can get and afford a sitter, the spontaneity is lost. And that goes for middle-of-the-afternoon lovemaking as well.

Sometimes you may get a sense that power issues have come to the fore as you and your toddler clash over who will control whom. There may be something "cute" about a defiant two-year-old, hands on hips, standing toe to toe with the parent who is insisting that it is time to get dressed to make a doctor's appointment. But there is nothing cute or fun about the reality of the power struggle that is in process. Your feelings of powerlessness may frustrate and infuriate you.

It would be unusual if any or all of these feelings were not stirred up, at least a bit, in any parent. We all remain vulnerable to the conflicts inherent in being and loving, even though we may think we have finally resolved them. However, it is what you *do* with these feelings that really matters—whether or not you can get a handle on them and put them in their proper perspective. After all, this twenty-month-old baby is not your mother or father, even though the feelings in you may date back to your struggle with them. This is a moment of potential growth for you—for the working through and resolution of the original problem.

Some parents, instead, try to defend themselves against their child in old ways, such as by withdrawing emotionally or by being overly compliant. Unfortunately, these solutions generate problems of their own. The withdrawing parent, in effect, abandons the child. The compliant and overly gratifying parent reinforces the infantile narcissism. Your own conflicts around being and loving may come to interfere with your capacity to parent your child in a way that will facilitate his or her development.

In addition to boundaries, autonomy, and power, issues of self-esteem may be raised in response to the child's impact on you. The behavior of our children can function as a mirror of ourselves. We may or may not like what we see. In their play and in their behavior they imitate both our positive and our negative aspects.[9] We feel good when we see the positive. We may feel unloved and angry when we see the negative. However, healthy parents can use the latter as helpful feedback, as a clue as to how the child experiences us in interaction with him. Then they can change their behavior toward the child for the better. If parents are to be able to use the child's behavior as information about the nature of their relationship, it is important that they not overemphasize the positive or be over-whelmed by the negative aspects of the self as they are exposed through the child's behavior. That is, our self-image and self-esteem should be secure enough to withstand such experiences. Parents who punish their children for behavior which they themselves have modeled not only do the child an injustice, but lose out on an opportunity for improving the relationship and for their own personal growth and maturation. One young mother was very angry with her little boy for hitting her and screaming at her when she did something he didn't like. It occurred to her that this was how he experienced her scolding and spanking, and she decided that her approach to discipline wasn't working. As she thought about it, she realized that she "disciplined" largely on the basis of her own mood, rather than consistently and in a way directly related to the child's behavior. As she was able to come to grips with what was going on within herself, she was able to change her way of handling her small son. Before long, his offensive behavior had dropped away.

It's not only important to understand your child and his developmental needs. It is equally important that you know and understand yourself so that you will be able to keep separate what has to do

9. Therese Benedek, "The Family as a Psychologic Field," in *Parenthood: Its Psychology and Pathology*, p. 127.

with you, and what has to do with him. For how you react to what comes from him will, in turn, affect him and how he is with you. The interaction continues to be one of mutual impact and response. You might find it useful to look back, as well, and to consider the impact you had on your parents and how this influenced the nature of your relationship. You were no more a lump of clay in their hands than your child is in yours.

RECIPROCITY—FOR BETTER OR FOR WORSE

How can the parent's conflict between being and loving affect a child's capacity to achieve these goals? There are many ways—some blatant and some subtle. Many have been described in this book.

The givens of the child are:

1. Its innate goal-seeking behavior in general and its attachment-seeking behavior in particular.
2. The mental organization of experience into patterns to which meaning is eventually assigned with the development of language. (One is the pattern called "self." Another is the pattern of the mothering person. These patterns are first organized before there is language and are carried forth into adult life to affect how we experience ourselves and others.)
3. Those functions that develop out of the biological maturation of the organism itself, such as walking, talking, thinking, perception, sexuality, and various inborn talents. (These functions develop within the context of the mothering environment. The quality of that environment determines whether they are associated with conflict and anxiety or whether they are free of conflict and can thus expand to their fullest and be enjoyed to their fullest.)

Whereas the capacity to love comes out of the attachment, being comes out of the integration of the many other innate and learned aspects of experience. These are significantly affected by the quality of the attachment bond and the nature of the relationship with the mothering person or persons.

As a parent, you may want to take a look at how the person you are is affected by these given aspects of your child and how the

PARENTS

CHILD	Ability to empathize and to respond to what comes from the child (*Your capacity to love*)	Capacity to tolerate your child's separateness from you (*Your capacity to be and for autonomy*)	Readiness to respect, respond to, and encourage your child's unique talents and abilities (*Your ability to relate to others as real and separate persons*)	Your ability to be a teaching parent and not feel guilty at setting limits and making appropriate demands (*Your sense of self and self-esteem*)
Attachment-seeking behavior	Capacity To Love			
Drive toward being separate	Capacity to Be	Capacity to Be		
Drive for autonomy	Capacity to Be Without Conflict	Capacity to Be Without Conflict	Self-Esteem	Mitigation of Normal Narcissism of Childhood and Promotion of Concern for Others
Unique temperament and abilities		Self-Expression, Pleasure in Achieving, and Self-Esteem	Self-Expression, Pleasure in Achieving, Self-Esteem	

OUTCOME FOR THE CHILD

person you are, in turn, affects or has affected these various aspects of your child's unfolding as a person.

You may recognize that some of the areas of your interaction with your child have not been exactly hospitable to either his growth as a person or to your own. Change in this respect can be difficult in that the system of how your family operates as an integrated whole tends to perpetuate the problems. This is why family therapy is often recommended as an approach to their resolution.

Problems of being and loving *within* each parent as they interact with problems of being and loving *within* each child can be looked at even as they are taking place. These interactions are both verbal and nonverbal, and the nature of the communication process is central to family therapy work. This is when someone who is outside of the family system can be helpful in changing it so that the individuals who make up the family can continue to grow as individuals. And as the negative aspects of the attachment bond can be resolved, family members can be freer to love one another in a nonhostile and nondependent manner. In effect, both being and loving will be enhanced.

You may want to attempt a few needed changes on your own. If your child or children are young enough, you may be able to turn the unhealthy relating around and get things moving in a more growth-promoting manner. If your children are older, this may not be so easy. I have observed many times that even as parents tried to change, children would pull them back into old ways of relating. For instance, if the parents tried to be less controlling, the child might provoke control in a variety of ways, such as using the new freedom to get even, to act out pent-up anger, or by playing inadequate and deliberately failing to carry out their part of the bargain. See if you can describe the interaction between you and your child under each of the following headings.

IS PERFECT PARENTING POSSIBLE?

The wish to be perfect and the tendency toward idealization of relationships becomes evident in the context of the family. The self-esteem of parents can get caught up in the need to be the perfect mother or the perfect father, and to have the perfect child to show to the world. To be a perfect parent and to have a perfect child is to be a perfect self. But, as in all other settings, perfection can only be an illusion which is maintained at the cost of denying reality.

The realities of the developmental process, with its inherent and inevitable conflict in the child between being and loving, as well as the parallel and related conflict between dependency and autonomy, automatically creates conflict between parent and child. There is no way any parent can avoid doing the "wrong" thing; no way to avoid being the "bad" one; no way to prevent disappointment and anger in the child; and no way to avoid completely some hurt to the child. In short, there is no way that one can be a perfect parent.

If a parent sides with the dependency, that aspect of the child that strives for autonomy will feel infantilized, controlled, and angry. If the parent sides with the autonomy, the aspect of the child that wants to be taken care of will feel abandonned, anxious, and angry. This kind of no-win parent-child situation can be observed with grown-up sons and daughters as well. Many men and women I have worked with are caught on the horns of this dilemma, and they cannot free themselves from the anger either. Eventually they must come to terms with the fact that it is they and not their parents who must take the ultimate responsibility for their being and loving, as well as for their dependency and autonomy needs. As long as the power is attributed to parental figures, they cannot move past the conflict. It is a dilemma that every parent will be caught up in no matter what he or she does or says.

Since perfection is impossible, what can be a reasonable and realistic goal for parents? How much can they ask of themselves?

PARENTING IN AN IMPERFECT WORLD

Having accepted the inherent imperfection in any parent-child relationship, one might hope at least that one could aim toward doing the most good and the least harm. But how can one know what course of action will meet even these requirements?

When in doubt, I find a useful rule of thumb to be that one should respond in a way that enables the child to function at his highest possible level at the moment, or that moves him gently forward.

It may be that easing the distress which is overwhelming him would do this. That is, responding to the dependency needs is indicated. At another time, it may be that encouraging the child to attempt some independent action is indicated. As long as he does not become overly anxious and unable to function, this will tend to be growth promoting, even though he may be irritated with you for not doing it for him.

Expressing loving feelings may make sense at a time when it clearly enhances the relationship and creates the good experience which eventually will become the child's inner source of nurturance. At another time, expressing one's displeasure will serve to mitigate the self-centeredness and enhance his awareness of others as important.

Sometimes you will guess wrong and have to deal with the consequences. Fortunately, children are very resilient and are able to tolerate many parental failures without being unduly damaged. Winnicott uses the term, "good-enough mothering." This can be expanded to "good-enough parenting." If parenting is good enough, the impetus to growth within the child makes its own contribution.

In general, promoting growth goes hand in hand with providing a safe resting place. If a child returns periodically to the haven of the lap, there is no need to be concerned about his dependency so long as he continues his excursions beyond the orbit of the parents with a modicum of success and manageable anxiety. Responding to his love, coupled with validation and support of his separate and autonomous self, will enhance his resolution of the conflict between being and loving. Knowing that he can experience both with you fosters the integration of the disparate aspects of his self. Later on with others, as he can now in his relationship with you, he will be able to "be me and love you."

THE WORKING MOTHER

What about the working mother? What of the woman whose own life as a person includes a career outside the home? It is not the intent of the writer to make her feel guilty or to justify the view of others who would have her stay at home and out of the work and professional world. Rather, my hope is to help her understand her own tremendous importance *as a mother,* and thus how to go about arranging to have her baby's needs met adequately in her absence.

There are two issues to be considered. The first and foremost is the fostering of the primary attachment bond with the mother herself. The second is the provision of the substitute caretaker, the mother surrogate.

The distinct psychological advantage of having the mother as the primary attachment figure is that she is most likely to be around for the duration of the growing years. This very continuity makes the psychological tasks of emotional development more readily managed by the child. Discontinuity, whether from day to day or from year to year, disrupts the smooth flow of the developing self in relation to another. This confronts the child with the sometimes insurmountable emotional task of having to deal with separation and loss.[10]

I have known a number of individuals who had made a primary attachment with a nursemaid who was dismissed from the family when the child was around three years old. Some of them continued to yearn for that which was lost to them. The lost nursemaid tended to be remembered as an idealized mother figure while the real mothers were experienced as cold deprivers of what had been so important to them. One woman felt that an important part of herself had been lost.

The working mother can foster the development of the primary attachment with herself by means of the quality of her interaction with her baby when she is at home. My own youngest child was born just as I was embarking on my professional career. The start and end of each day were special times for our being together. Feeding, bathing, playing, tucking him into his crib at night and singing his special songs—they all created the interpersonal ambience that enabled me to be away during the day and, at the same time, to foster this important developmental process.

Arranging for substitute caretaking for your child should be undertaken with the care it deserves. Responsible mothers generally look into the reliability, cleanliness, and kindness of a sitter or of teachers at a nursery. The factors of *continuity* and *stability* may not be considered as carefully.

A predictable and familiar world facilitates the process of organization, attachment, and of assimilating new experiences into a growing, integrated view of the self and the world. Disruptions of the child's life—and this includes discontinuous and unstable substitute mothering arrangements—may have their counterpart in the disruption of these processes.

Douglas's mother is a teacher. He stays at a community nursery while she is at work. He is an especially bright and responsive child. In her journal his mother described him as happy to go to school,

10. John Bowlby, *Attachment and Loss,* vol. 1 (New York: Basic Books, 1969).

loving his teacher, and as being friendly and cooperative with the other children. At home he was affectionate, lively, and developing emotionally as one might anticipate for his age.

When Douglas was almost two years old, his mother put him into a different nursery during the summer when his regular one was closed. He began to scream every day when she left him there, started to hit the other children, and became tense, wild, and uncooperative at home, often striking out at his mother. He also developed a sleep problem. When it became evident that he could not cope with the disruptive stress of the new situation, his mother kept him at home, and he soon resumed his previous healthy course of development. He was able to return to the familiar nursery and teacher once again in the fall with little more than some initial clinging.

The child is particularly vulnerable to the effects of disruptions of its world in the first three years of life. The working mother, cognizant of her child's developmental needs, can foster the attachment bond and arrange for not only good but stable substitute caretaking. She can create for him an interpersonal world that will facilitate the capacities for both being and loving.

BIBLIOGRAPHY

Benedek, Therese. "The Family as a Psychologic Field," in *Parenthood: Its Psychology and Psychopathology,* edited by E. J. Anthony and T. Benedek, pp. 109–35. Boston: Little, Brown, 1970.

Bergmann, Martin S. "Psychoanalytic Observations on the Capacity to Love," in *Separation-Individuation: Essays in Honor of Margaret S. Mahler,* edited by John McDevitt and Calvin Settlage, pp. 15–40. New York: International Universities Press, 1971.

Bowlby, John. *Attachment and Loss,* vol. 1. New York: Basic Books, 1969.

Bry, Adelaide. *60 Hours That Transform Your Life.* New York: Avon, 1976.

Erikson, Erik. *Childhood and Society.* 2nd ed. New York: Norton, 1963.

Erikson, Erik. *Identity: Youth and Crisis.* New York: Norton, 1968.

Fantz, R. L. "The Crucial Early Influence: Mother Love or Environmental Stimulation?" *American Journal of Orthopsychiatry* 36, no. 2 (1966): 330–31.

Festinger, L., Riecken, H. W., and Schacter, S. *When Prophecy Fails.* Minneapolis: University of Minnesota Press, 1956.

Foulkes, David. *The Psychology of Sleep*. New York: Scribner's, 1966.

Freud, Anna. "The Concept of Developmental Lines," in *The Process of Child Development*, edited by Peter Neubauer, pp. 25–45. New York: Aronson, 1976.

Goldberg, Susan, and Lewis, Michael. "Play Behavior in the Year-old Infant: Early Sex Differences." *Child Development* 40, no. 1 (1969): pp. 21–31.

Handel, Gerald. "Sociologic Aspects of Parenthood," in *Parenthood: Its Psychology and Psychopathology*, edited by E. J. Anthony and T. Benedek, pp. 87–105. Boston: Little, Brown, 1970.

Harlow, Harry. "Early Social Deprivation and Later Behavior in the Monkey," in *Unfinished Tasks in the Behavioral Sciences*, edited by A. Abrams, H. H. Garner, and J. E. P. Toman. Baltimore: Williams and Wilkins, 1964.

Horner, Althea. "Self-deception and the Search for Intimacy." *Voices* 6, no. 2 (1971): 34–36.

Kaufman, Charles. "Biologic Considerations of Parenthood," in *Parenthood: Its Psychology and Psychopathology*, edited by E. J. Anthony and T. Benedek. Boston: Little, Brown, 1970.

Kohut, Heinz. *The Analysis of the Self*. New York: International Universities Press, 1971.

Kohut, Heinz. *The Reconstruction of the Self*. New York: International Universities Press, 1977.

Lichtenberg, Joseph D. "The Development of the Sense of Self." *Journal of the American Psychoanalytic Association* 23, no. 2 (1975): 453–84.

Mahler, Margaret S. *On Human Symbiosis and the Vicissitudes of Individuation*. New York: International Universities Press, 1968.

Mahler, Margaret S., Pine, Fred, and Bergman, Anni. *The Psychological Birth of the Human Infant*. New York: Basic Books, 1975.

Maslow, Abraham. *The Farther Reaches of Human Nature.* New York: Viking Press, 1971.

May, Rollo. "The Emergence of Existential Psychology," in *Existential Psychology,* edited by Rollo May. New York: Random House, 1965.

May, Rollo. *Love and Will.* New York: Norton, 1969.

May, Rollo. *Man's Search for Himself.* New York: Dell, 1973.

Miller, Arthur. *I Don't Need You Any More.* New York: Viking, 1967.

Minuchin, Salvador. *Families and Family Therapy.* Cambridge, Mass.: Harvard University Press, 1974.

Morgan, Marabel. *The Total Woman.* New York: Simon and Schuster, Pocket Books, 1975.

Plato. *Symposium,* Great Books of the Western World, vol. 7, p. 158. Chicago: Encyclopaedia Britannica, 1952.

Roback, H. B., and Abramovitz, S. J. "Deterioration Effects in Encounter Groups." *American Psychologist* 31, no. 3 (1976): 247–55.

Rutter, Michael. *The Qualities of Mothering: Maternal Deprivation Reassessed.* New York: Aronson, 1974.

Schafer, Roy. *A New Language for Psychoanalysis.* New Haven, Conn.: Yale University Press, 1976.

Spitz, René. *The First Year of Life.* New York: International Universities Press, 1965.

Thomas, Alexander, and Chess, Stella. *Temperament and Development.* New York: Brunner/Mazel, 1977.

Tolpin, Marian. "On the Beginnings of a Cohesive Self: An Application of the Concept of Transmuting Internalization to the Study of the Transitional Object and Signal Anxiety." *The Psychoanalytic Study of the Child,* vol. 26. New York: Quadrangle Books, 1971.

Winnicott, D. W. *The Maturational Processes and the Facilitating Environment.* New York: International Universities Press, 1965.

Winnicott, D. W. "Primary Maternal Preoccupation," in D. W. Winnicott, *Through Paediatrics to Psycho-Analysis*, pp. 300–305. New York: Basic Books, 1975

Wolfe, Tom. "The 'Me' Decade and the Third Great Awakening." *New York* magazine, August 23, 1976, pp. 26–40.

INDEX